Global E-Litism

Digital Technology, Social Inequality,
and Transnationality

Contemporary Social Issues

George Ritzer, *Series Editor*

Contemporary Social Issues

Series Editor: George Ritzer, University of Maryland

Global E-Litism

Digital Technology, Social Inequality, and Transnationality

Gili S. Drori

Stanford University

Worth Publishers

Acquisitions Editor: Erik Gilg
Executive Marketing Manager: John Britch
Associate Managing Editor: Tracey Kuehn
Project Editor: Penelope Hull
Art Director: Babs Reingold
Text Designer: Lissi Sigillo
Cover Designer: Lyndall Culbertson
Photo Editor: Ted Szczepanski
Production Manager: Sarah Segal
Composition: Matrix Publishing Services
Printing and Binding: RR Donnelley
Cover photo: Yellow Dog Productions/The Image Bank/Getty Images

ISBN 0-7167-5673-0   (EAN: 9780716756736)

© 2006 by Worth Publishers

Printed in the United States of America

First printing 2005

Worth Publishers
41 Madison Avenue
New York, NY 10010
www.worthpublishers.com

To Ulli, Teta, and Boo for their love and patience
and to Jer for his never-ending support and encouragement

About the Author

Gili S. Drori received her Ph.D. in sociology from Stanford University and is currently a lecturer in Stanford University's programs on international relations and international policy studies. Her research interests include the comparative study of science and technology, social progress and rationalization, globalization, governance, and higher education. She is the author of several papers and chapters on science and development, world culture, international organizations, and governance, as well as a coauthor of *Science in the Modern World Polity: Institutionalization and Globalization* (Stanford University Press, 2003).

Contents

x Contents

Foreword

As we move on in the twenty-first century, we confront a seemingly endless array of pressing social issues: urban decay, inequality, ecological threats, rampant consumerism, war, AIDS, inadequate health care, national and personal debt, and many more. Although these problems are regularly dealt with in newspapers, magazines, and trade books and on radio and television, popular treatment has severe limitations. By examining these issues systematically through the lens of sociology, we can gain greater insight into them and be better able to deal with them. It was to this end that St. Martin's Press created this series on contemporary social issues and that Worth Publishers has chosen to continue it.

Each book in the series casts a new and distinctive light on a familiar social issue, while challenging the conventional view, which may obscure as much as it clarifies. Phenomena that seem disparate and unrelated are shown to have many commonalities and to reflect a major, but often unrecognized, trend within the larger society. Or a systematic comparative investigation demonstrates the existence of social causes or consequences that are overlooked by other types of analysis. In uncovering such realities the books in this series are much more than intellectual exercises; they have powerful practical implications for our lives and for the structure of society.

At another level, this series fills a void in book publishing. There is certainly no shortage of academic titles, but they tend to be introductory texts for undergraduates or advanced monographs for professional scholars. Missing are broadly accessible, issue-oriented books appropriate for all students and for general readers. The books in this series occupy that niche somewhere between popular trade books and scholarly monographs. Like trade books, they deal with important and interesting social issues, are well written, and are as jargon free as possible. However, they are more rigorous than trade books in meeting academic standards for writing and research. Although they are not textbooks, they often explore topics covered in basic textbooks and therefore are easily integrated into the curriculum of sociology and other disciplines.

Each of the books in the "Contemporary Social Issues" series is a new and distinctive piece of work. I believe that students, serious general readers, and professors will all find the books to be informative, interesting, thought provoking, and exciting. Among the topics to be covered in forth-coming editions in the series are the declining wealth and increasing in-debtedness of the middle class and the risk-taking nature of contemporary Americans.

—George Ritzer

Preface

In November 2005, Tunisia hosts the second phase of the World Summit on Information Society (WSIS). In this forum, government ministries, corporations, nongovernmental organizations, and grass-roots associations all display their contributions to and achievements in advancing the cause of the information society worldwide. The first phase of WSIS was held in Geneva, Switzerland, in December 2003, and since then several agencies, primarily the International Telecommunication Union (ITU), have monitored the progress of countries and international bodies in achieving the goals specified in the Declaration of Principles and a Plan for Action of WSIS.

WSIS is indeed an impressive display of international concern with the worldwide diffusion of advanced technology, with the use of technology for development, and with the still obvious fact that the vast majority of humanity has not been touched by the digital revolution. WSIS conveys a sense of hope: in halls and conference rooms, dignitaries and delegates repeat the mantra of the tremendous opportunities for development set in motion by the digital revolution and offer creative ways to reach every village and every city slum and every school and every peasant the world over with cutting-edge technological innovations.

It was difficult, in this period of hopeful initiatives, to write this book. It is difficult to hold onto the view that information is not in itself a magic cure for hunger, poverty, and illiteracy. It is hard not to see this latest UN initiative in the context of previous—and mostly failing—plans that highlighted education, science, and human capital as the necessary bases for human progress. It is challenging to avoid putting this technological inequality into the context of social inequality in general and thus regarding it as yet another dimension of social hierarchy with every one of the markers of social marginality. For these are the themes of this book: the technological and global dimensions of social inequality as new dimensions of an old social ailment and consideration of the Internet within the context of its social, and particularly cultural, roots.

Acknowledgments

I was working on issues of the globalization of science when George Ritzer approached me to write this book. At the time, very few studies explored advanced technology from a sociological and comparative perspective, and fewer still could empirically document the trends of high-tech globalization. George Ritzer granted me an exhilarating opportunity to venture into this emerging field of study; he also skillfully molded my writing in the field. I thank him for this support and inspiration.

My first steps in exploring the issue of global technological inequalities and in dealing with the methodological shortcomings were done with Yong Suk Jang. I thank him for his ideas and hard work in applying institutional lessons from the fields of education and science to the brave new world of high tech. I thank John Meyer and Chiqui Ramirez for their continuous support and encouragement throughout this long journey; our shared work on globalization has shaped this manuscript. I thank Emily McKenzie and Eric Kramon for skillfully and patiently executing the data research for this book and Susan Wyle for reviewing my writing. I thank Erik Gilg and the three reviewers for Worth Publishers for urging me to sharpen my ideas and hone my arguments. And I especially thank Penny Hull for her dedicated scrutiny of my composition and insightful comments on the content.

The people dear to me were obviously involved, too. I thank my friends Hadar Shemtov, Alex Gerbasi, and Jerry Sanders for guiding my writing by commenting on early versions of the manuscript. Jerry's creativity came up with the book's title. My parents' photographs from their travels here and there gave me the idea for the book's cover. Most of all, I thank my kids for patiently bearing with me through the distraction I go through while writing.

Introduction

In the winter of 1995, the *New Yorker* magazine published yet another of its astute commentaries on the current state of our lives. This time, it was a cartoon showing a graveyard, with the closest gravestone engraved "RIP@deadasadoornail.com."[1] This *New Yorker* cartoon was saying that these days even the dead have an e-mail address or that there is no escape from the Internet, and thus it highlighted a world changed by the fast-advancing technology of the Internet. The sense of rapid sociotechnological changes was also evident in my household, where my young daughters could draw with a mouse with more precision and control than they could with a crayon. The Internet age has seemed to overwhelm every aspect of our lives and its expansion has led to a common complaint about departure from the security of familiar patterns. Our lives have indeed changed dramatically with the proliferation of e-technology: we rely on it to expedite human communication, thus exchanging more information more intensely and faster. Through e-technology, we also extend our human networks into new spaces, thus establishing more contacts with more people and institutions. We experience a condensation of social space, linking with people and cultures far away and far removed from us. We are members of the "network society."[2]

Plenty has been written on the "fabulous nineties" and the high-tech boom. Most pieces take a business perspective and contemplate the still untapped potential of the Internet and related technologies. They describe technological change as a venue for unleashing human potential and a source for rapid advancement; they consider technology as a means for development and its acquisition as a matter of corporate and national strategy. The goal of this book is to depart from the business point of view to offer a sociological perspective on the social role and impact of high tech in the current era. In this sense, I will review and consider classic sociological dimensions of technology and society:

♦ How is technology diffusing? What are the patterns of technological diffusion? What are the barriers to the free diffusion of technology?

♦ Who owns the technology and why? How will technology be used to identify social classes or cleavages?

♦ What are the perceptions of technology that conceal its stratifying effects in an era of talk of equality and distributive justice?

I do not ask the question Where do human inequalities—specifically technological inequalities—come from? Obviously, they come from unequal access to other social resources, such as income and education, from availability of electricity and broadband connection, from language skills and societal support. The interesting point is, in my mind, the tracing of the features of inequality and the discussion of its lingering effects on the human future. These indelible features of inequality and their persistent effects are labeled by Charles Tilly "durable inequalities." Tilly defines them as inequalities that "last from one social interaction to the next, with special attention to those that persist over whole careers, lifetimes, and organizational histories."[3]

Social inequality is not a metaphysical notion or an abstract sociological concept; rather, it describes a bewildering array of concrete dimensions along which access to social resources (from work, to family ties, to language, to technology) is differentiated. In this book I focus on the intersection of technology and social stratification, and because recent technological changes have had a large global or international component, I am particularly interested in technology and stratification on a global scale. I therefore consider in this work to be about the relationship between technology creation and diffusion, on the one hand, and global social inequality, on the other. I argue that the diffusion of technology follows the contours of social groups: new technology is first diffused among the rich, educated, well-connected, and globally mobile social groups, while the penetration of new technology among the poor and disenfranchised is dramatically slower. Most important, the contours of social groups are not random; rather, they follow the social demarcations of wealth and other social "resources," from education to gender to race to residency.

Intersecting Technology and Inequality: The Global Digital Divide?

Since the language of social stratification, or inequality, is not the dominant one in discussions of high tech, I am devoting this section to explaining my focus on the intersection between technology and inequality. The relationship between the pair of notions was codified as the "digital divide"; the coining of this phrase is attributed to Larry Irving, who oversaw the writing of the 1999 report "Falling through the Net" in his role as the assistant secretary for communications and information in the U.S. Department of Commerce during the Clinton administration. More work is now emerging on the digital divide in the United States,[4] but little of it investigates the global dimensions of the divide. Whereas most of the scholarship on the global digital divide takes the viewpoint of development economics or technical matters,[5] I intend to shed a sociological light on the discussion of the work on the comparative or cross-national digital divide. The following discussion explains this sociology of the global digital divide by confronting the catchy title for this emerging body of literature on the cross-national case of technology and inequality: the global digital divide.

Why "Divide"?

Stratification is a classical theme in sociology: since the early days of the discipline, it has been clear that social activities of diverse sorts have varied greatly in intensity among members of society. The "sociological eye" identifies these social differences as neither random nor accidental; rather, social differences reflect a system of social stratification or a systematic hierarchical ranking of social groups into social classes or strata. Whether such strata are defined by economic capital, human capital, cultural traits, or inherent features, the patterns are clear and simple, if not obvious: there are differences in behavior and action, as in life style and life chances, between rich and poor, educated and uneducated, black and white, men and women, as well as along the lines of ethnic, religious, occupational, age, and generational demarcations. And these groups are organized hierarchically, with one characteristic (within each stratifying dimension) marked as desirable and thus rewarded: whites are privileged over blacks, men over women, and white-collar workers over blue-collar workers. The core intellectual and research agenda is, then, to identify the dimensions along which societies are stratified and to describe the relevant sources and the consequences of the inequality. In other words, a core disciplinary concern is with the factors that map the stratification system onto differential access to social resources.

The clear patterns of differential access to and use of social resources mean that inequality is institutionalized. Institutionalized inequality translates to patterns of inequality or social exclusion being accepted and practiced as the custom of the land—and in some countries even set in discriminatory rules of the state. In this sense, social exclusion is different from inequality or deprivation. Rather than treating social exclusion as an inert social condition, the inequality approach focuses on the dynamics of the social process and on the mechanisms that operate to perpetuate it. Most important, these differences are consequential for future prospects: the boundaries of social strata are the boundaries of our social opportunity structure. And the more firm and unyielding the stratification system is, the more limited are the horizons of social opportunity for the members of the lower strata, or the disenfranchised groups. Because of these obvious implications, the discussion of inequality is a core concern not only to social scientists but also to policy makers. This concern is rooted in the modern thinking that equates inequality with injustice.

Do these patterns constitute discrimination? And if so, who is behind this discriminatory scheme? On these issues social scientists debate fiercely. Classic opinions stretch from the functional theory of stratification (the most notable thinkers are Kingsley Davis and Wilbur E. Moore), which asserts that hierarchical stratification is organized around social needs and differential skills to satisfy the needs, and Karl Marx's class distinction by material power between the "haves" and the "have nots," to the more nuanced Weberian thinking about status groups as derived from the combination of prestige and political access, in addition to material power.[6] Across these visions of social differences and explanations of their roots is, however, a shared sociological understanding of inequality as a core feature, if not prism, of social life.

Why "Global"?

Social interaction is intensely global: the era of globalization is marked by the expansion of social exchanges internationally and transnationally. Global interaction extends to more and more spheres of our life. These days, people, commodities, capital, and information rapidly flow across national borders and to all hidden corners of the world. The age of globalization also added to these global contacts the consolidation of global tastes (in fashion and foods) and global images (of heroes and villains, of civil and savage, of modern and backward). Globality, then, describes the scope of social life.

Globality is now in every sphere of social life: economic, political, environmental, cultural, and legal, as well as security, identity, and nationality. The trend of globalization has also introduced new social players into social interactions, from multinational corporations to international non-governmental organizations and transnational social movements. The age of globalization has stretched the boundaries of society beyond the "nation" and "state citizenship" to the global. We now engage in social interactions around the physical space of the globe, we regard global actors as relevant to our life, and we stretch our loyalties to reflect our new status as "citizens of the world." Consequently, we also regard social problems and social injustice to be global in nature. Environmentalism, or care of the natural environment, is considered a global problem of ecological dependency; human rights violations are measured by global moral codes; and programs for alleviation of poverty in remote parts of the world demonstrate concerns with deprivation and misery on a global scale.

More specifically, the core theme of this book is not inequality per se but rather centrality/marginality: the degree of involvement in and influence over social life. Moreover, I am interested in global centrality/marginality as it is marked and highlighted through the prism of digital technology. By the transnational nature of this new technology (because of the sort of social contacts that it enables), centrality/marginality is also transnational in character. As Saskia Sassen notes, the new spatial arrangement in the e-age results in the "neutralization of place and distance through telematics."[7] There is, then, no longer a tight link between geographical location and centrality: the e-economy, even when glorifying and then emulating the regional success of Silicon Valley, is neither centered in Silicon Valley nor controlled from other tech hubs in Sweden or Bangalore or financial centers such as Wall Street or London's City. Indeed, a part of this new spatial rearrangement is the "running away" of global cities, urban locales that are the junctions of global contacts and transactions. Yet these new global centers are also meta-geographical. They are linked with each other more than they are to their national and geographical proximities; they are thus linked and disconnected through e-contacts and digital technology. Cyberspace is a new and virtual space for social contacts and transactions, and it is essentially global. Cyberspace is, then, the ultimate technoscape, or the new landscape of cultural and political activity that is shaped by technology, to use the language of Arjun Appadurai.

The new notion of space of social life, or -scapes, is now also global. Appadurai identifies six sorts of new social fields, labeled by the suffix "-scape": ethnoscape, mediascape, financescape, ideoscape, and technoscape.[8] In each scape, globalization has caused a deterritorialization of what was once considered local, particular, and authentic. The global distribution of ideas and images, as well as of their formal expressions in social policies, results in the condensation of time and space dimensions into an intensely unified global condition or existence. Anthony Giddens sees such condensation of time and space as the prerequisite for the modernizing process of disembedding, or "the 'lifting out' of social relations from local contexts of interaction and their restructuring across time and space."[9] The geographer David Harvey adds that the time–space compression, which means that people stationed in different parts of the world can experience the same event (such as a media event or a telephone call) at the same time as if sharing one location, has resulted in the annihilation of space by time compression. He illustrates this point by drawing world maps in different time points, proportionally representing social tasking on a temporal–spatial dimensions, showing that the world in 1960, even before the digital communication revolution, was one fifth the "size" of the world of the sixteenth century.[10] This notion of shrinking of time and space is well expressed in the following MCI Telecommunications commercial: *There will be no "there." We will all be here.*[11]

The interesting item in these new arrangements of social time and space is that they are both unifying and differentiating (in Michel Foucault's language, both totalizing and individualizing) and that these seemingly contradictory tendencies occur simultaneously. So when it comes to space and to notions of centrality/marginality, the recent tendencies of concentration and dispersal are seemingly contradictory yet complementary at the same time. On the one hand, concentration is the growing transfer of control of financial, cultural, and military power to a few global cities. Moreover, this era is marked by political unipolarity and a rampant neoliberal ideology, both strengthening a single (global) image of appropriateness. On the other hand, vertical integration of production networks allows global dispersal of production sites; thus, prosperity comes to the global margins. Overall, then, information and communication technology (ICT) has a central role in creating these seemingly contradictory totalizing/individualizing tendencies. New technology has shrunk the world by intensifying social contacts while also spreading the wings of global production to create enclaves of the e-economy outside the developed core and thus bring greater differentiation and inequality to these global ends. This new technology, then, is simultaneously a global unifier and a global divider.

Why "Digital"?

The latest dimension to be added to the nuanced demarcation among social groups is technology. Whoever masters technology is considered more modern and highly developed; whoever controls advanced technology is considered more powerful and influential. The focus on technology as an important social resource is not new; the digital age has merely magnified previously conceived concerns about the role of technology in social stratification. As William Gibson, the noted creator of the cyberpunk genre, is believed to have said: "The future is already here. It's just not very evenly distributed."[12]

The tale of the International Telecommunication Union (ITU) exemplifies this new twist to an old concern: each year on May 17, ITU celebrates World Telecommunication Day to commemorate its founding in Paris in 1865. Over the past decade, this event has drawn growing attention and has become particularly symbolic: the era of globalization and the age of the telecommunication revolution have focused the attention of world audiences on matters of information and communication technology. "Internet" and "e-commerce" have become the "buzz words" of policy makers and industry leaders, if not common household language. In the words of Neil Selwyn, "Information and communication technology is the indispensable grammar of modern life and a fundamental aspect of citizenship in the ensuing information society."[13] In this sense, the reason for us to focus the discussion of social inequality on technology is the heightened importance awarded to technology in the age of globalization and the era of the high-tech boom. Advanced technologies, specifically information and communications technologies such as the Internet and cellular phones, have come to symbolize this era more than anything else. These technologies mark the advances in global connectivity, and for social scientists they also mark the contours of global marginality. Arjun Appadurai's "technoscapes" means a rearrangement of social contacts through and by technology. Technoscapes transcend traditional barriers of nation and state by connecting people across the world by their common mastery of technology: kids from elite families meet in chat rooms, well-known Internet engineers meet at professional conferences, high-end consumers shop on e-commerce sites. At the same time, these technoscapes are also exclusionary mechanisms: they exclude all those who lack access to ICT or basic skills to use ICT or who perform only basic functions with ICT.

Is this new digital technology different from older ones? Does the new digital technology mark this era in ways that are different from the ways by which earlier periods, such as the Industrial Revolution, were marked by the technological advances of their times? The conceptual link between technology and development is well established and longstanding: human-made technology is considered the basis for social development. As a result of this conceptual link, we mark social eras by the technological capacity of the time, from the iron age to the space age. Yet in spite of this conflation of old-style technologies with the recent high-tech boom and the link now established with old-style telecommunication, the technologies that are the markers of the global digital divide are unique and their effects on social stratification are very powerful.

While we commonly use "e" to stand for various electronic technologies, it is most commonly used to refer to digital technologies and lately to the Internet. In general, however, "digital" refers to a wider range of technologies that rely on a similar storage and transmission technology.

This storage and transmission technology is based on binary or dichotomous (as opposed to analog or continuous) coding of data. The data are stored and transmitted as a sequence of discrete symbols from a finite set and are represented using electronic or electromagnetic signals.[14] Included among these technologies are, then, computers,[15] cellular telephones,[16] facsimile machines,[17] digital photography, music and video DVDs, as well as, of course, the Internet and World Wide Web. These devices rely on digital data to make storage and transmission more effective and clear, then convert or translate these digital signals into approximations of analog signals to make the human–machine interface easier; the conversion is done in the interface between hardware and software—the gadget and its "brain" or operating system. For example, our PC keyboard allows us to write in English, while the machine records our alphanumeric codes into digital ones. Our CD allows us to hear music in the full range of notes and octaves while it reads these nuances of sounds from a digital code because it digitizes to a resolution that exceeds perceptible limitation in print or sound. This means that although we the users no longer recognize each digital machine as digital, the core technology is digital.

These technologies, while all technically defined as digital, vary in the degree of impact they have on social life. Since my work focuses on the social dimensions of new technology, I am narrowing my definition to solely information and communication technologies (ICT). I am therefore leaving out of my discussions digital technologies and devices that are components of the device that is actually used as an ICT. (See Box 1.1 for descriptions of the devices.) I do not describe or address technologies such as CDs and DVDs (compact discs and digital versatile disks that allow data storage), chips and semiconductor processors (required to operate the devices), or other components of these technologies (such as a mouse, printer, or modem). Rather, I focus on the information and communication technologies of computers and the Internet; I also occasionally address the technologies of cellular phones and facsimile machines. In general, all these devices share the technical definition of digital technology insofar as they are also sharing the goal of facilitating communication.

Another common feature of ICTs is that they have dramatically changed social interaction: they have intensified exchanges and have expanded the distance of such exchanges. As mentioned earlier, they are responsible, more than any other factor, for the condensation of time and space dimensions in the latest era. Information—from factory orders to personal letters to news—travels faster and connects farther-away places more than ever before. The importance of this technology to social change goes to our notion of the nature of being: ontologically, these digital technologies also carry the hope of bringing development. In this sense, the technol-

Box 1.1

What's in a Name?

ICT (*information and communication technology*) is a new name for a series of digital technologies whose main use is in information (storage, retrieval, and dissemination) and communications (exchanges, connections, and relations). Until recently—2000 or so—the standard label for these technologies was IT (*information technology*). Before that, the common names were *informatics* and *telematics*. Why this change of the name for the same set of technologies, and what is the meaning of the change? I see this change of the name as reflecting the process of peopling of the technology.

Informatics, used interchangeably with *information science,* refers to computer and statistical techniques for data, their management, and their manipulation. The focus is on data and on the science of managing data. The 1990s term *information technology* treats data as information and moves away from the scientific features of its management; the power of data came to be understood as being drawn from the information they provide to policy and planning. In this sense, the focus shifted away from science and data toward the social uses of information. The now common term ICT treats the relevant technology as a means of exchange, thus adding a social interaction dimension to the technique itself.

This change in language to describe the same group of technologies reflects the process of the peopling of technology: technology is made relevant to the people who use it. This is a discursive shift from an emphasis on the technical matter to an emphasis on social uses. The purpose of the technology is not to celebrate itself (its achievements and its development in a scientized and expert-based manner) but rather to serve people (as clients, as communities).

ogy is intended to change our lives and our relations with other people in ways that are neither casual nor for entertainment. Overall, therefore, "e" or "digital" stands for the notion that the latest of human technologies have profoundly affected human life, changing our daily habits, building new and dissolving old human communities, changing the interaction between humans and nature.

Although digital technology builds on a few decades of other scientific and technical advances and although it varies from pagers to computers to cellular phones and stretches between the software and the hardware for all these gadgets, the important matter for this discussion of the global digital divide is that digital technology marks the frontier of technical advances to date. As the frontier, or cutting edge, digital technology is hailed as holding the potential to foster economic development and to reduce inequality. As such, it encompasses the potential for human creativity and the hope for contribution and advancement. When this promise is broken, through revealing social inequalities rather than closing the gaps, the disillusion from the meliorist role of technology in society is great. Technology was always considered a source of hope and also a marker for social divides; now, in the high-tech age, both hope and divide are more intense.

The digital age is a global age in more than the mere extent of our expectations for humanity. This era is a global era not merely because digital technology is shrinking and spanning the globe. As Bruce Kogut states in his introduction to an edited volume on the global Internet economy, the global reaches of the technology provide the enabling and powerful factors in its diffusion, yet not the necessary factors.[18] Rather, digital technology—and thus the social divides that it creates—is the ultimate global technology because global actors were its main motors of diffusion. Global, mostly transnational, actors—from multinational corporations to international governmental and nongovernmental organizations—all supported the buildup of digital technology and encouraged its diffusion. For all of them technology was a core goal, and for all of them globality was a means to achieve their goal, from WIPO's[19] regulatory control over intellectual property rights and ICANN's[20] coordination power over domain names to Intel Corporation's "around the clock development" strategy and UNESCO's promotion of technological literacy in schools. In this sense, globality and digital technology are intertwined: the development of the technology is entangled with the intensification of globalization and with the work of global organizational players.

A Short History of the High-Tech Time

In 1982, *Time* magazine altered its annual tradition of naming a "Man of the Year," choosing instead to name the computer "Machine of the Year." In introducing the theme, *Time*'s publisher, John A. Meyer, wrote, "Several human candidates might have represented 1982, but none symbolized the past year more richly, or will be viewed by history as more significant, than a machine: the computer."[21] This was a formal recognition of a technological change that had already left an indelible mark on social life by 1982: the rapid innovation in the field of digital technology, from materials and software to communications, that established digital technology and the computer as its emblematic symbol as clearly marking a new era for humanity.

It was clear then that in spite of the short duration since the seeds of this revolution were planted, this age is like no other technology-based social revolution. The main difference is the rapid rate of change: the rate of development and of diffusion of digital technology is faster than that of any other communication technology before it. The Internet, for example, was adopted by American households more quickly than any other prior technological innovation, faster than cell phones and personal computers and much faster than other household products such as the microwave, VCR, and telephone.[22] Also, in the United States as in Japan, the rate of adoption of the Internet in large businesses was faster than that in households; by 2000, 95.8% of all Japanese business enterprises used the Internet.[23] And the usability of the Internet accelerated the purchases of PCs as household items: by 2000, 59% of American households owned a PC and 51% owned more than one PC. This fantastic rate of adoption of computer technology into households and businesses meant a shortening of the duration of building up a market for the products and the duration of building a users' community for each product. "It took television 13 years and the telephone 75 years to acquire 50 million users," while "it took the internet [only] five years."[24] Clearly, the expansion of the Internet confirms both "Moore's law," which predicts the doubling of computing power every 18 months, and "Gilder's law," which forecasts the doubling of telecommunications power every 6 months (Box 1.2).

Box 1.2

Moore's Law and Gilder's Law

Both "laws" concern the rapid rate of technological progress in the ICT field. "Moore's law," based on a 1965 observation made by Gordon Moore, Intel's cofounder, states that the number of transistors per integrated circuit grows at an exponential rate; Moore also predicted that this trend would continue. This means that data density, or processing power, doubles approximately every 18 months. Moore's original statement was made a mere four years after the first planar integrated circuit was invented, but the law stands valid to this day. Most important, Moore's law sets the expectation for the industry. The accuracy of the prediction and the historical regularity of semiconductor progress became the standard expectation for the pace of innovation in the field.

In 1993, George Gilder, a technotheorist, observed that in bandwidth the rate of progress is much faster than originally predicted by Moore: specifically, transfer capacity is expected to rise at a rate three times the rate at which processing power is increasing, or three times the rate of Moore's law. In other words, while processing power doubles every 18 months, bandwidth will double every 6 months. This assessment, first published in an article in *Forbes ASAP* in 1993 and later restated in Gilder's 1996 book *Telecosm*, was titled "Gilder's law." It too was found to be true: currently, bandwidth capacity doubles every 4 months.

This high-tech era is made particularly distinct by several features: the intense rate of innovation and diffusion, the extra premium for technology as a measure of achievement, and the webbing of a new economic sector, coupled with great disparity. Although the latter issue—the social disparity that is perpetuated by this new technology—is the core of this book, let me reflect now on the development of the field, which brought many celebrated products and benefits to our times.

The Boom: Amazing Innovation and Diffusion

The 1990s are forever marked by the high-tech boom: the rapid rate of innovation in the field of high tech and the amazing rate of structuration of the e-economy. "E-" and ".com" seemed to be the lingo of the day in the 1990s. But the boom of the 1990s and its popularization of digital technology rested on a few decades of technical progress in the field of electronic and material engineering and on the blossoming of the fields of software and computer sciences.[25]

The first computer, named ENIAC[26] and designed by John Mauchly and J. Presper Eckert, was completed and first displayed to the public in 1946. With its blinking lights, cards, and switches, it reached a speed of 5,000 operations per second. It also occupied 1,000 square feet of floor space and weighed over 30 tons.[27] ENIAC was commissioned by the U.S. military with an immediate use in mind: to enable quick and complicated ballistic calculations. The initial contract, dated June 5, 1943, committed $61,700 in U.S. Army Ordnance funds and called for six months of "research and development of an electronic numerical integrator and computer and delivery of a report thereon."

This humble beginning was fueled by a vision of the potential of these computational systems. Leading the visionaries was Vannevar Bush, the man who later founded the Defense Advanced Research Projects Agency (DARPA) and cofounded Raytheon (the largest military contractor in the United States). In July 1945, in an article in the *Atlantic Monthly*, Bush wrote:

> Consider a future device for individual use, which is a sort of mechanized private file and library. It needs a name, and to coin one at random, "memex" will do. A memex is a device in which an individual stores all his books, records, and communications, and which is mechanized so that it may be consulted with exceeding speed and flexibility. It is an enlarged intimate supplement to his memory.

It consists of a desk, and while it can presumably be operated from a distance, it is primarily the piece of furniture at which he works. On the top are slanting translucent screens, on which material can be projected for convenient reading. There is a keyboard, and sets of buttons and levers. Otherwise it looks like an ordinary desk.[28]

The memex idea inspired a generation of scientists and engineers who kept searching for an application for this idea in the field of electronics.

Most of the subsequent work in computer development took place in the University of Pennsylvania's Moore School of Electrical Engineering. By October 2, 1955, at 11:45 P.M. (when the plug was literally pulled on ENIAC, its work was taken over by the more powerful EDVAC and ORDVAC, and the Department of Defense contracts were terminated), ENIAC's applications had expanded to include weather prediction, atomic energy calculations, cosmic ray studies, thermal ignition, random number studies, wind tunnel design, and other scientific uses. Experimentation with computers had taken root. Computers became aids in various high-computational work that extended beyond military uses to encompass a variety of public needs.[29]

These early steps in digitization and computation mark a revolutionary point in the history of technology: the digitization of input, or the concept of software, made possible the transformation of the machine's utility from one domain to another. The machine became by definition programmable and thus not dedicated to any one sort of product or assignment. By opening up the versatility of the machine and its uses, digital technology changed the playing field of technology.

Rapid advances followed, learning from ENIAC's limitations and advancing its qualities. For one thing, ENIAC was an "energy hog." Reportedly, its power needs—with its 17,468 vacuum tubes, 70,000 resistors, 10,000 capacitors, 1,500 relays, and 6,000 manual switches—resulted in brownouts in its host city of Philadelphia. Yet at the same time, ENIAC and the work on its development and use propelled additional ideas in the field. In 1949, Maurice Wilkes, a Cambridge University faculty member who spent several years at the Moore School, designed and assembled EDSAC,[30] the first practical stored-program computer.[31] The importance of EDSAC to the field lies in its programming: Wilkes established a library of short programs called subroutines stored on punched paper tapes and reused for parallel tasks.

In addition to technical advances, the field of computers made its first steps toward professional recognition and toward software development during the early 1950s. Maurice Wilkes, in collaboration with colleagues from Cambridge University, published in 1951 the first book on programming (titled *The Preparation of Programs for an Electronic Digital Computer*), and in the same year Cambridge University started offering a diploma in numerical analysis and automatic computing. Although the academic program was merely a one-year postgraduate course, it was the first formal course leading to a university qualification in computing anywhere in the world. Also that year, Engineering Research Associates of Minneapolis built the ERA-1101, the first commercially produced computer, holding 1 million bits on its magnetic drum. The company's first customer was the U.S. Navy.

The year 1956 also bore important milestones. At MIT, the first transistorized computer, the TX-O,[32] was completed, and in November IBM introduced the RAMAC 305, the first hard drive, with 50 two-foot diameter platters and a total capacity of 5 MB. With the additions of a keyboard and a monitor (first added to the PDP-1 minicomputer, offered by Digital Equipment Corporation in 1957 for US$120,000) and a "mouse," or pointing device for computers (invented by Douglas Engelbart at Stanford Research Institute—SRI—in 1963), the computer grew to have all the basic components that we recognize today.

Since then, though, the field of computers has progressed dramatically on all fronts and computers have become smaller, faster, and more capable. On the engineering front, a few technical transitions made progress in leaps and bounds: the transition from transistors to integrated circuits (first introduced in 1964 in IBM's System/360); the transition from the magnetic core memory of Jay Forrester's 1953 Whirlwind computer to the development of semiconductors in the 1970s; and the transition from magnetic disk storage (which began with IBM's shipment of a 305 RAMAC to Zellerbach Paper in San Francisco in 1956) to Intel's rapid advances on microprocessors in the 1970s. With these transitions, computers quickly grew in power. IBM's Stretch was outpowered by Cray's supercomputers (the first 6600 model was introduced in 1964 and Cray-I, its first powerful commercial unit, was offered in 1976). The computer became more personal: Hewlett-Packard's first general-purpose computer, the HP-2115 (1996—the first small-frame high-computational power unit that supported a wide variety of languages), was quickly replaced by General Corporation's Nova (1968—32 kilobytes of memory for a mere $8,000), by the short-lived Kenbak-1 (1968—advertised for $750 in *Scientific American*), and by the Alto (1974—developed at Xerox PARC, it ran several files simultaneously on windows and had a built-in mouse and linking to a local network). The result was not only a powerful PC, but a PC that was "user friendly": the mouse and windows set-up allowed interface through "point and click" (rather than through cumbersome programming) and multitasking.

On the software side, Claude Shannon's 1948 coinage of the term "bit" as the fundamental unit of data and computation was followed by the introduction of such now well-known names in computer language as FORTRAN[33] in 1957, COBOL[34] in 1960, and the encoding system ASCII[35] in 1963. UNIX, introduced in 1969 by AT&T Bell Laboratories program-mers Kenneth Thompson and Dennis Ritchie, was a successful and widely used multiuser, multitasking operating system. And the 1981 launching of MS-DOS,[36] the basic software for the newly released IBM PC, established a long partnership between IBM and Microsoft. By 1983, Microsoft, which was established by Bill Gates and Paul Allen in 1975, announced Word in 1983 and Windows in 1985[37] and became pivotal to the popularization of the PC as a consumer product.

Once computers took hold within corporations and households, great opportunities lay ahead for those who commercialized these gadgets. In 1983, Compaq Computer Corporation introduced the first PC clone that used the same software as the IBM PC. With the success of the clone, Com-paq recorded first-year sales of $111 million, the most ever by an Ameri-can business in a single year. With the introduction of its PC clone, Com-paq launched a market for IBM-compatible computers that by 1996 had achieved an 83% share of the personal computer market. The other share of the market was held by Apple Computer's Macintosh, a highly graph-ical computer launched in 1984 for $2,500; it came to be known as the "anti-PC." Overall, by 2002 1 billion PCs had shipped worldwide, making the PC into the most popular of the ICT devices.

These technical advances and commercial opportunities spawned a wave of incorporations: new firms, sponsored by venture capital, took root, es-pecially around university campuses. Corporations adopted the "Silicon Valley model" worldwide, and the model's founding fathers quickly adapted to new competition and new technological advances. "Old" names such as IBM and Hewlett-Packard meshed with the 1980s Cisco Systems, Sun Mi-crosystems, and Oracle to create a dense network of organizations that to-gether composed the new e-economy.[38] And the use of computers—for of-fice operations and later in e-sales—penetrated even established and traditional companies to create "click and mortar" companies: the shipping company FedEx offered its customers an on-line tracking system for deliv-ered packages, store-based companies like General Motors and Wal-Mart re-lied on sophisticated EDI (electronic data interchange) systems to keep track of stock and facilitate shipments, and mail-order and phone-order retail companies such as Eddie Bauer and Land's End quickly offered their cata-logues and ordering services on-line.[39] Overall, then, the technology pen-etrated old and traditional corporations and grew a new sector of startups.

The last sphere of computer advances was in networking, or connec-tions among computers and stations. The early work aimed at creating a global open network of electronic information exchange was done in DARPA[40] laboratories in the early 1960s. These early experiments with the notion of a "galactic network" evolved into the 1968 development of ARPANET[41] and later the introduction of "internetting." In September

1969 the first Internet server was installed at UCLA, rapidly followed by installations at Stanford University, the University of California at Santa Barbara, and the University of Utah. Still, the development of the Ethernet at Xerox PARC in the 1970s and used to refer to the family of local-area networks (LANs), started the storm of linking computers up to accelerate capacity and to exchange information. These experiments with open-architecture networking[42] and with various protocols to meet the requirements made by the openness resulted in the Internet of the 1990s. In 1989 Tim Berners-Lee developed the basic concept of the World Wide Web while at the European Organization for Nuclear Research (CERN), and the concept was strengthened by the 1993 introduction of Mosaic[43] and the 1994 launch of the World Wide Web Consortium.[44] This groundbreaking project developed a global hypertext platform for information sharing, making the Internet into an information and communication bridge across businesses, peoples, and governments the world over.

These technical advancements meant that the capacity of advanced digital technology "exploded" during a rather short period. The Internet, for example, is dramatically more robust than any other computer system: "In 2001 more information [could] be sent over a single cable in a second than in 1997 was sent over the entire Internet in a month."[45] International Internet capacity reached the remarkable level of some 300 Gb/s in 2001, almost five times greater than its capacity in 1999 and exceeding international telephone circuit capacity.[46] With this delivery capacity grew storage capacity and interest: the number of Web sites grew from 200 in June 1993 to 20 million in late 2000,[47] with estimates of as many as 2 million Web pages added daily.[48] The number of Internet hosts worldwide doubled in the two years 1999–2001[49] and grew tenfold[50] in member states of the Organisation for Economic Co-operation and Development (OECD) between 1990 and 2000.[51]

In summary, digital technology developed on several distinct planes, all of which intertwined to create a new era. Together, developments in the fields of electrical and material engineering, software, and networking created the new and sophisticated digital gadgets. And a new discipline emerged to train students for the relevant professions: as mentioned earlier, the first degree-awarding program in the discipline that came to be known as computer science was established at Cambridge University in 1951. As a result of these technical and professional developments, a new economic sector consolidated, comprising both manufacturing and communications, while the old manufacturing sector adopted the gadgets to enhance its productivity.

Throughout this period of development and expansion, digital technology also changed all parameters of technology diffusion previously conceived of, and the Internet, which appeared on the field of communication technology only in the mid-1990s, sped the rate of diffusion even more. Digital technology, and particularly its latest offspring, the Internet, made unprecedented leaps in terms of accessibility and affordability; the Internet has spread to consumers and users far more quickly than previous technological advances, and it is lower in cost than all other communication and household technologies before it. Digital ICT, then, quickly lowered the barriers to technology usage. During its short life, Internet technology has enabled more people to have access to more information at a lower cost than imagined or planned by its conceivers. Nevertheless, numerous barriers still prohibit most of humanity from access to ICT, tainting the impressive technological accomplishment with the notoriety of widening social gaps.

Left behind the Boom

The impressive records of diffusion of ICT are marred by huge gaps in the social groups that could access these technologies. So although advanced digital technology is spreading worldwide at the fastest rate of any technology diffusion ever and thus reaching more people faster, there are still plenty of people for whom this technology is a remote dream. This stunning juxtaposition is a telling fact about our modern condition: at a time when we are celebrating dramatic rates of technological diffusion and are preaching a culture of inclusion, we are seeing striking rates of inequality. As an illustration, consider the revealing comparison between (a) the gross exponential rates of growth in overall usage and (b) the breakdown of these general rates by the level of economic development. Figure 1.1 shows the rapid rate of growth in the number of PCs and in the number of Internet users worldwide between the late 1980s and 2002. The rates of change in total usage were exponential: the rate of change in PC ownership was doubling every two or so years, and the growth rate for the number of Internet users was even faster. Figure 1.1, then, traces a magnificent picture of global technological diffusion, rapidly spreading gadgets and their use to consumers worldwide.

This image of rapid diffusion, which to some implies greater accessibility of ICT, conceals the drama of social inequality. Rather than simply considering the worldwide overall growth, consider where around the world the phenomenal growth has taken place. Figure 1.2 breaks down the data presented in Figure 1.1 by national wealth. Specifically, the worldwide data

Figure 1.1

The Magnificent Picture of High-Tech Diffusion

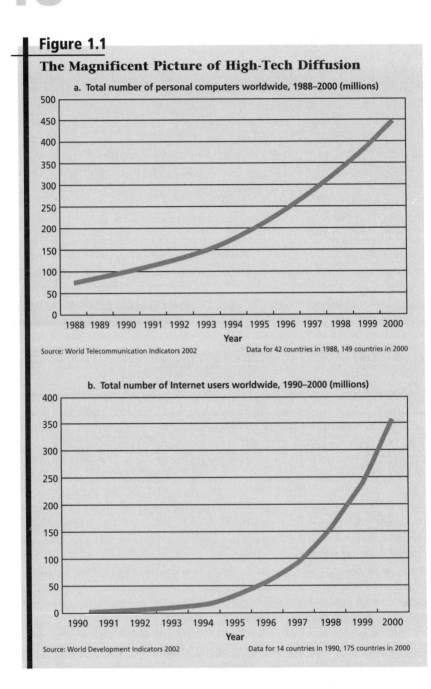

a. Total number of personal computers worldwide, 1988–2000 (millions)

Source: World Telecommunication Indicators 2002   Data for 42 countries in 1988, 149 countries in 2000

b. Total number of Internet users worldwide, 1990–2000 (millions)

Source: World Development Indicators 2002   Data for 14 countries in 1990, 175 countries in 2000

Figure 1.2

Breakdown of Total Numbers by Three-Category National Income

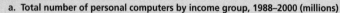

a. Total number of personal computers by income group, 1988–2000 (millions)

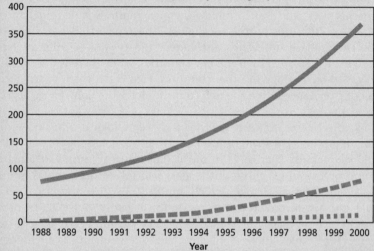

Source: World Telecommunication Indicators 2002
■ ■ ■ Low income: 4 countries in 1988, 44 countries in 2000
▬▬ ▬▬ Middle income: 16 countries in 1988, 67 countries in 2000
▬▬▬ High income: 22 countries in 1988, 36 countries in 2000

b. Total number of Internet users by income group, 1990–2000 (millions)

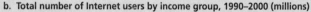

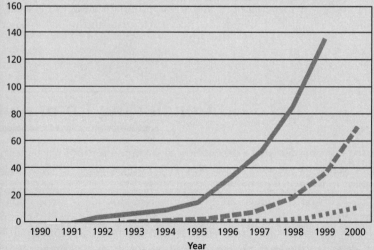

Source: World Development Indicators 2002
■ ■ ■ Low income: 1 country in 1990, 59 countries in 2000
▬▬ ▬▬ Middle income: 5 countries in 1990, 70 countries in 2000
▬▬▬ High income: 22 countries in 1988, 36 countries in 2000

are broken into three groups of countries based on World Bank categorization of national income: low-income countries, middle-income countries, and high-income countries. This look at the same data reveals troubling trends that continue today. Most of the world's Internet users and most of the world's PCs are in high-income countries, while the number of Internet users and PCs in middle-income countries is marginal and in low-income countries is truly negligible. The rates of change since the 1980s are similarly unevenly distributed: the celebrated rates of rapid change tell the story in high-income countries, while there is little change in access to technology in other countries. Figure 1.2, then, charts for us a map of global inequality: the rich countries have the lion's share of computer technology.

This comparison between the views of technological diffusion brings up the questions "How should we be measuring technology?" and "How should we measure change?"[52] It seems that this may simply be a matter of opinion: Should we consider the glass half full or half empty? Should we focus on rates of change, which are on some dimensions greater in middle- and low-income countries, or on the disparity in overall use or use per capita? These questions are at the core of debates about poverty and strategies for its alleviation: neoliberals consider inequality as a temporary phase corrected by utility and market needs, while critical social scientists regard inequality as a marker for persistent social injustice and seek to change its institutional roots. This debate will be raised throughout the following discussions. The conceptualization of social inequality, the role of technology in social change, and the appropriate means to correct inequality are repeated challenges for social scientists and policy makers.

Concluding Comments

I started this chapter with a description of sweeping technological changes as they seemed to readers of the *New Yorker* magazine in 1995: an image of rapid and pervasive changes in our daily lives. Let me conclude the chapter with another image, an image prevalent around the world in places far removed from the global core. The picture on the cover of this book is of a Masai warrior in Africa. He is standing somewhat defiantly in full tribal dress and body markings, leaning on his spear. The image is symbolic of traditional Africa. But towering above him, in the far distance, are satellite dishes, an image symbolic of Africa's future.

This picture clearly dramatizes problems of development, revealing a world that mixes decrepit conditions with the cutting-edge means; it expresses the dissonance of development in many world regions where computer technology is penetrating but where basic living conditions are archaic. Problems of development are intertwined with issues of technology diffusion: computers can be used only in places that are connected to an electrical grid and Internet access is possible only on PCs that are connected through a modem to a telephone system. Utility infrastructure and thus development are, then, necessary components of technology access and technology use; without this infrastructural backbone, still absent for 85% of the world population, there is no future for high tech and its connectivity.

In addition to the understanding of infrastructure as a prerequisite to any technological advance, I hope the picture also invokes in you what I see as a sociologist: a juxtaposition of "high" and "low" technology working side-by-side and simultaneously. This is a picture of the contradictions of development, not to say the dialectics of capitalism, allowing social progress and social regression to coincide.

The new age of ICT, enhanced and enhancing rapid globalization, created these seemingly contradictory combinations: a PC delivered on a donkey, a computer lab in a school with no blackboard, a satellite dish mounted on a mud hut. It wraps these contradictory tendencies in the veil of the hope of progress: social change, if not revolution, comes on the back of technological progress, even when elementary means and conditions are absent. Just as during previous social revolutions, hopes of progress are interwoven with the despair of perpetuated inequality. And in the age of globalization, this concern has been reoriented to focus on global inequality and world-scale disparities. During the age of globalization, then, world-scale disparities in access to new and advanced technologies chart for us a new global human geography.

Notes

1. Mick Stevens, *New Yorker* cartoon 13592.
2. The term "network society" was coined by Manuel Castells in his seminal series of volumes on the information age published by Blackwell (Oxford and Malden, MA): Volume 1, *The Rise of the Network Society* (1996); Volume 2, *The Power of Identity* (1997); Volume 3, *End of*

Millennium (1998). See also Jan Van Dijk (1999), *The Network Society* (London: Sage).

3. Charles Tilly (1999), *Durable Inequalities* (Berkeley: University of California Press), p. 6.

4. Examples of recent edited volumes on the American digital divide are Benjamin M. Compaine (ed.) (2001), *The Digital Divide: Facing a Crisis or Creating a Myth?* (Cambridge, MA: MIT Press); Pipa Norris, W. Lance Bennett, and Robert M. Entman (2001), *Digital Divide: Civic Engagement, Information Poverty, and the Internet Worldwide* (Cambridge, UK: Cambridge University Press); Karen Mossberger, Caroline J. Tolbert, and Mary Stansbury (2003), *Virtual Inequality: Beyond the Digital Divide* (Washington, DC: Georgetown University Press).

5. Examples are Jeffrey James (2003), *Bridging the Global Digital Divide* (Cheltenham, UK: Edward Elgar); Mitsuhiro Kagami, Masatsugu Tsuji, and Emanuele Giovannetti (eds.) (2004), *Information Technology Policy and the Digital Divide: Lessons for Developing Countries* (Oxford, UK: Marston); Bruce Kogut (ed.) (2003), *The Global Internet Economy* (Cambridge, MA: MIT Press).

6. For a review text of all classical sociological approaches to stratification, see David B. Grusky (ed). (1994), *Social Stratification: Class, Race, and Gender in Sociological Perspective* (Boulder, CO: Westview Press).

7. Saskia Sassen (1996), "The Spatial Organization of Information Industries: Implications for the Role of the State," in James H. Mittleman (ed.), *Globalization: Critical Reflections* (Boulder, CO: Lynne Rienner), p. 35.

8. Arjun Appadurai (1996), *Modernity at Large: Cultural Dimensions of Globalization* (Minneapolis: University of Minnesota Press).

9. Anthony Giddens (1990), *The Consequences of Modernity* (Cambridge, UK: Polity), p. 21.

10. David Harvey (1989), *The Condition of Postmodernity* (Oxford: Blackwell), p. 241.

11. Quoted in Malcolm Waters (1995), *Globalization* (London: Routledge), p. 124.

12. Quoted from NPR's *Talk of the Nation,* November 30, 1999.

13. Neil Selwyn (2002), "E-Stablishing an Inclusive Society? Technology, Social Exclusion and UK Government Policy-Making," *Journal of Social Policy* 31: 1–20.

14. We still count volume in digital technology in terms of the number of binary switches. "Bit" stands for *binary digit*, and eight bits equal a byte (as in megabyte—1 million bytes—or gigabyte—1 billion bytes).

15. Computers vary greatly by their capacity—their size and computational power. They range from personal computers or workstations

(single-user computers) to mainframes (multiuser systems) and super-computers (extremely powerful systems).

16. Digital cellular technology combines digital transmission of various sorts, such as Global System for Mobile Communications (GSM) and Code-Division Multiple Access (CDMA), with cell geographical allocation of communication networks.

17. Abbreviated to "fax machine," the facsimile machine digitizes an image and transmits the digital information through telephone connections. The idea of dividing an image into a grid of dots and then assigning digital codes to each such dot came from Alexander Bain's work in 1842 and from a patented device named "a copying telegraph" by a London inventor named F. C. Blakewell in 1850. This technology was popularized only in the mid-1980s, thanks to the establishment of a standard set by the Comité Consultatif International Télé-phonique et Télégraphique (CCITE), now a part of ITU; specifically, the initial standard is called "group 3" protocol and it allowed communication between sending and receiving devices).

18. Kogut (2003), note 5, p. 33.

19. The World Intellectual Property Organization (WIPO) is a member of the United Nations' system of organizations. It administers 23 international treaties dealing with different aspects of intellectual property protection.

20. The Internet Corporation for Assigned Names and Numbers (ICANN) is a not-for-profit organization established in 2000 to take over from the hands of the American Internet Assigned Numbers Authority (IANA) the powers of assigning Internet domain names and numbers. ICANN registers the domain name system and the Internet protocol address and manages the Internet's domain name server (DNS) system.

21. John A. Meyer (1983, October 5), "Machine of the Year," *Time*.

22. See Compaine (2001), note 4, p. 322, and Norris et al. (2001), note 4, p. 33.

23. Mari Sako (2003), "Between Bit Valley and Silicon Valley: Hybrid Forms of Business Governance in the Japanese Internet Economy," in Kogut (2003), note 5, p. 295.

24. Linda Main (2001), "The Global Information Infrastructure: Empowerment or Imperialism?" *Third World Development* 22(1): 85.

25. For a chronology of advances in digital technology, see the Appendix.

26. ENIAC stands for Electronic Numerical Integrator Analyzer and Computer.

27. ENIAC's size, once a matter of design and capacity, is now a barrier to its adequate recognition and preservation. Although numerous

agencies recognize its role as an icon symbolizing the latter half of the twentieth century and the triumph of technology, few can display it in full. As a result, some of ENIAC's parts are on display at the United States Military Academy at West Point, New York, as an emblem of military technology, and other ENIAC components are awaiting placement at the Smithsonian Institution and corporate headquarters.

28. Vannevar Bush (1945, July), "As We May Think," *Atlantic Monthly*, pp. 101–108.

29. Sources: http://ftp.arl.army.mil/~mike/comphist/96summary/ and http://ftp.arl.mil/~mike/comphist/eniac-story.html, accessed April 14, 2003.

30. EDSAC stands for Electronic Delay Storage Automatic Calculator. See http://www.cl.cam.ac.uk/UoCCL/misc/EDSAC99/, accessed April 14, 2003.

31. For a first-hand account of these first experiments, see M. V. Wilkes (1985), *Memoirs of a Computer Pioneer* (Cambridge, MA: MIT Press).

32. TX-O stands for Transistorized Experimental Computer.

33. FORTRAN stands for *For*mula *Trans*lator.

34. COBOL stands for Common Business Oriented Language.

35. ASCII stands for American Standard Code for Information Interchange.

36. MS-DOS stands for Microsoft Disk Operating System.

37. Only in 1990 did Microsoft ship Windows 3.0, which was the first successful version of Windows for PC users.

38. See Kogut, note 5.

39. See Martin Kenney (2003), "The Growth and Development of the Internet in the United States," in Kogut (2003), note 5, pp. 86–87.

40. DARPA, the Defense Advanced Research Projects Agency, is the central R&D organization of the U.S. Department of Defense.

41. ARPANET was the first network operating with interface message processors (IMPs).

42. In open-architecture networking, the network links multiple independent networks through an arbitrary design and does not force a protocol or technology on them.

43. Mosaic was the first popular graphic interface for the World Wide Web.

44. See Berners-Lee's tale of the invention of the World Wide Web: Tim Berners-Lee (with Mark Fischetti) (1999), *Weaving the Web: The Original Design and Ultimate Destiny of the World Wide Web by Its Inventor* (San Francisco: Harper).

45. United Nations Development Programme (2001), *Human Development Report 2001: Making New Technologies Work for Human Development* (New York: UNDP), p. 30.

46. International Telecommunication Union (2001), *Numbering Cyberspace: Recent Trends in the Internet World* (ITU, Telecommunication In-

dicators Update, January/February/March). http://www.itu.int/ITU-D/ict/statistics, accessed October 31, 2002, p. 3.

47. UNDP (2001), note 45, p. 32.

48. Quoted in Paul DiMaggio, Eszter Hargittai, W. Russell Neuman, and John P. Robinson (2001), "Social Implications of the Internet," *Annual Review of Sociology* 27: 308.

49. The number of Internet hosts grew from 72,004,971 in 1999 to 141,382,198 in 2001. See http://www.itu.int/ITU-D/ict/statistics/at_glance.

50. The number of Internet hosts grew from 9.1 per 1,000 people in 1999 to 98.1 per 1,000 people in 2000.

51. United Nations Development Programme (2002), *Human Development Report 2001: Deepening Democracy in a Fragmented World* (New York: UNDP), p. 189.

52. These questions may also be conceived of as technical questions: What indicators better reflect trends in ICT diffusion from a comparative perspective? I reconcile this technical debate with data about several ICTs that are available cross-nationally and over time. Throughout this book I demonstrate arguments with various indicators, trying to avoid single-indicator bias and trying to consider whether trends are similar across specific measures.

The New Global Geography

"Today's world is divided not by ideology but by technology," argues Jeffrey Sachs.[1] Sachs makes the case that global divides are no longer about beliefs, ideas, and principles; rather, global divides are along the lines of the ownership, creation, and utilization of technology. The old label *geopolitics* is, then, replaced these days with *geotechnologics*: interstate alliances and international status of nations and corporations are marked today by the access, use, and control of technology; geography has less and less influence over the social future. The principle of international arrangements has not changed: the global organization of labor and the alliances of trade and politics still clearly trace spatial arrangements. What changed in the 1990s is the criterion for international arrangements: spatial arrangements were reset along the lines of technological capacity.

To trace the global diffusion of technology and its differential rates of absorption worldwide, then, is imperative for understanding our social world. Tracing the spatial differentiation of technology also delineates social groups, social dynamics, and social institutions: through the prism of technology we can distinguish the poor from the rich, the elite from the disenfranchised, and the engaged from the marginalized. Similarly, we can map processes of status closure or convergence of these social groups through the prism of technology. We can record the institutions of education, of the workplace, of trade, and regard them as markers of status attainment. And, as argued earlier, in the age of globalization the tracing of advanced technology and its social impacts are similarly on a global scale. In this chapter I trace the differential access and use of ICT; I also trace technological achievements as the markers of development; and I parallel the achievements with some notes on technological *under*achievement.

Fact Sheet of the Global Digital Divide

As reviewed earlier, the growth in the capacity of advanced digital technology is most impressive, and the Internet's rate of growth, in particular, is like that of no other technology before it. For example, the number of Internet users around the world grew from 16 million in 1995 to over 500 million in 2001. The number of e-mail accounts grew from about 15 million worldwide in the early 1990s to 569 million at the end of 1999;[2] the number of countries connected to the Internet grew from 8 in 1988 to 214 in 2003;[3] and the number of secure Internet hosts worldwide grew to 217,255 by 2003.[4] Clearly, the Internet has been adopted by American households more quickly than any other prior technology, faster than other digital technologies or other ICT media. As cited earlier to describe the rapid rate of adoption: "It took television 13 years and the telephone 75 years to acquire 50 million users," while "it took the internet [only] five years."[5] This phenomenal growth was concentrated in the 1990s: the worldwide average number of Internet users (per 1,000 people) rose from 0.5 in 1990 to 131 in 2002.[6] Since the autumn of 2001, the growth of the Internet has somewhat slowed down, especially in the United States and Europe; in the developed countries, fewer users have come on-line and some users have gone off-line.[7]

The rapid technical advances in the ICT field mean that some barriers to the technology's diffusion are dissolving or at least being lowered dramatically. Such barriers are, most obviously, in terms of the technology's capacity and of its cost. First, the greater the capacity of digital technology, the more tasks it can perform, leading to its greater desirability to customers. According to Moore's and Gilder's laws, the computational power and the networking power of the computer grow exponentially. In addition, technical advancement in technology also means cheaper access to it: for example, the cost of one megabit of computer memory dropped from US$5,257 in 1970 to only US$0.17 in 1999,[8] and Internet dial-up costs[9] reached their lowest rate ever in 2002—an average of US$45 for 30 hours of dial-up access in the 30 member countries of the Organisation for Economic Co-operation and Development (OECD).[10] With these rapid technical changes and the lowering of cost and capacity barriers, ICT became the new economic hope for advancing nations: in 1999, 52% of Malaysia's exports, 44% of Costa Rica's, 28% of Mexico's, and 26% of the Philippines' were from the high-tech sector.[11] India's revenue from the ICT sector jumped from US$150 million in 1990 to US$4 billion in 1999, but action has slowed down dramatically since the third quarter of 2001.[12]

Still, despite these changes in access to and cost of communication brought about by advances in digital technology since the late 1970s, many people worldwide are "falling through the net."[13] Even the Internet's rapid growth in usage did not alter the extent of its global reach: only 5% of the world's population is now on-line.[14] This disparity in technology extends to technology creation: OECD countries, which are home to only 14% of world's population, account for 91% of the total of 347,000 or so new patents issued in 1998,[15] 86% of the total 863,000 patent applications field in 1998, and 85% of the 437,000 scientific and technical journal papers published worldwide.[16] In R&D terms, OECD countries invest an average 2.4% of their GDP in R&D, while the average for Asian countries is 1.6% (ranging between 1.1% in Singapore and 2.8% in South Korea[17]). These numbers reflect an uneven ownership of intellectual property and thus of future benefits from technology creation. Of the worldwide royalty and licensing fees in 1999, two countries alone account for 66% of these fees: 54% went to the United States and 12% went to Japan.[18]

Still, the most dramatic markers of access to digital technology are the global wealth and regional divides. More than 97% of all Internet hosts, which indicate the capacity of the local ICT sector to deliver service, are located in developed countries that are home to only 16% of the world's population.[19] By comparison, in 2000, 35 of the least developed countries that were home to half a billion people accounted for only 1% of on-line users.[20] Clearly, if digital technology were equally diffused worldwide, across state borders and social divides, then each country and each world region would have a share of technology use in the same proportion as its share of the global population. But obviously, the comparison of the share of the world's population by category with the share of the population slice that has access to digital technology exposes the biased distribution of digital technology.

This biased distribution of ICT is not random but rather systematic. This pattern of technological inequality has clear social markers, specifically, wealth and world location. Although I explore the issue of the social markers of the global digital divide in great depth in Chapter 3, here I wish to highlight some of the dominant features. Most clearly, access to digital technology is systematic by wealth. For example, great differences in the proportion of access exist between three groups of nations, differentiated by their national income. As indicated in Figure 2.1, high-income countries, as a group, have the lion's share of Internet users. And although middle-income countries are increasing their share in the world digital market and low-income countries are finally getting even the smallest share in the digital community, these shares are by far smaller than their population share.

Figure 2.1

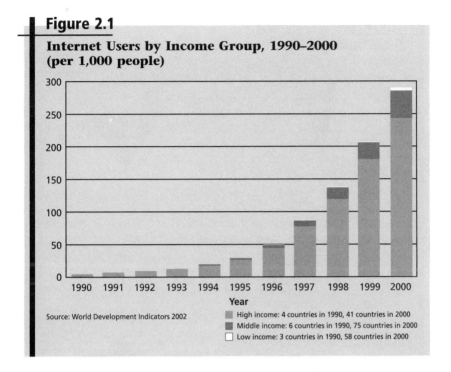

**Internet Users by Income Group, 1990–2000
(per 1,000 people)**

Year

Source: World Development Indicators 2002

High income: 4 countries in 1990, 41 countries in 2000
Middle income: 6 countries in 1990, 75 countries in 2000
Low income: 3 countries in 1990, 58 countries in 2000

Similarly, great differences in access to digital technology exist across world regions: 79% of the world's Internet users are citizens of OECD countries, which are home to only 14% of the world's population;[21] in sub-Saharan Africa, only 0.4% of the population uses the Internet. Even in India, a hub for the emerging e-economy, the share of Internet use is only 0.4% of the population.[22] As indicated in Figure 2.2, the share of high-income OECD countries overwhelmingly dominates the global landscape of digital technology use. Although the relative share of PC ownership by these rich countries is on the decline, they still hold some 85% of the world's PCs while accounting for only 14% of the world's population.

These nations—demarcated by wealth or world region—are not totally homogeneous in rates of access to and use of digital technology. Rather, great variation in use of digital technology stretches *within* groups of countries, even among the developed and affluent nations. Again, although I describe the social features that distinguish these groups of nations in Chapter 3, I allude here to some of the overall trends. Clearly, even within the group of OECD member nations, the difference among countries is dramatic: in the year 2000, for example, the number of Internet hosts per

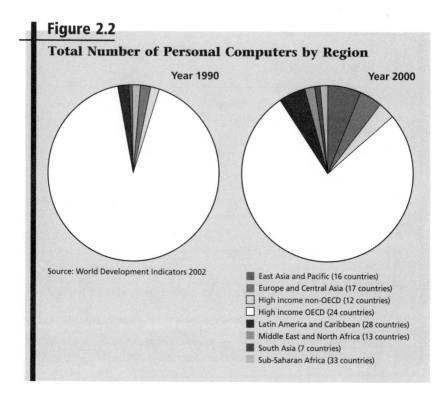

Figure 2.2

Total Number of Personal Computers by Region

Year 1990   Year 2000

Source: World Development Indicators 2002

- East Asia and Pacific (16 countries)
- Europe and Central Asia (17 countries)
- High income non-OECD (12 countries)
- High income OECD (24 countries)
- Latin America and Caribbean (28 countries)
- Middle East and North Africa (13 countries)
- South Asia (7 countries)
- Sub-Saharan Africa (33 countries)

1,000 people in Finland, the United States, and Norway was 200.2, 179.1, and 193.6, respectively, whereas the ratios in other OECD countries were much lower: in Japan, Germany, and South Korea the ratios were 49.0, 41.2, and 40.8, respectively.[23] Similarly, Internet dial-up costs among OECD countries stretched between some US$90 per 30 hours in June 2000 in Belgium and US$13 in Canada.[24] Moreover, while Scandinavian countries rank highest in all per capita measures of Internet use—51.5% of their population is on-line[25]—the United States is clearly the world leader: 79% of all Internet hosts, 59% of all electronic mailboxes, 54% of all on-line shoppers, and 38% of all Internet users are American. These data reveal the extent of differences in Internet access, capacity, and cost, even within this exclusive group of economically advanced and technologically sophisticated countries.

Even if the map of social causes reveals an intricate web of contributing factors, from heritage to language and gender barriers, it is clear that these worldwide gaps stem directly from two main sources: the availability of infrastructure and the cost of the technology. First, the North–South divide results from differences in infrastructure and thus in capacity: for example, the whole continent of Africa has less bandwidth than the city of Sao Paulo, Brazil, while Latin America's total bandwidth is roughly equal to that of the city of Seoul, South Korea.[26] Similarly, Hong Kong and Tokyo together have 1/50 of the bandwidth of the United States; furthermore, this gap in bandwidth capacity extends also between Hong Kong and Tokyo and all other Asian main cities. In this sense, it is infrastructure that enables or prohibits access to ICT: in countries and world regions that lack capacity, digital connections are less efficient and, by definition, less available. In this sense, varying levels of Internet capacity set barriers before ICT users in developing countries and in marginal regions: their network is overloaded, if not overwhelmed, not because of a large number of users or great amounts of data transferred but because of a low capacity to serve users. It is, therefore, the lack of capacity of the local network that blocks locals from fully utilizing ICT.

A second barrier to full use is cost. Mainly due to income differentials, ICT—hardware, software, and connection—is too expensive for average people and thus it is beyond the reach of most locals. For example, in 2000 the cost of a single PC in the United States equaled 1/10 of the GDP per capita, while in Zimbabwe the cost of a PC equaled about 10 times the GDP per capita.[27] Similarly, in 2000 the United States monthly Internet access fees were 1.2% of the average monthly income; in the rest of the world the costs were dramatically higher: in Sri Lanka the ratio of access fee to income was 60%, in Bhutan 80%, in Bangladesh 191%, in Nepal 278%, and in Madagascar the monthly Internet access fees were equal to 614% of the average monthly income.[28] Therefore, with average annual income in low human development countries equaling US$1,200, owning the cheapest Pentium III computer costing about US$700 in January 2001[29] and maintaining an Internet connection were still distant dreams for most of humanity. With these rates for acquiring access to ICT, it is evident that most of the world's population still cannot afford this technology and is therefore barred from its advantages. After all, most of humanity is struggling to afford basic life necessities like food, clothing, and medication; only half of humanity has ever made even a single phone call.[30] These people certainly cannot afford the expense of purchasing the necessary technological tools (like a PC or a cellular phone) or paying the connection fees (of either the phone to a phone system or the PC to an ISP for Internet use).

In summary, while the world is clearly more digital, persistent patterns of technological marginality remain: core countries are more wired than marginal countries, people in rich countries have more extensive access to and use of digital gadgets than do people in poor countries, and citizens of Western countries are more tech-savvy than people of all other countries. And although the marginalized world is catching up with some technologies, the patterns of global technological marginality are growing. It is these global social divides, which map onto the parameters of technological marginality, that define the global digital divide. Moreover, it is these social parameters that make what is sometimes referred to as a technical matter of technological efficiency and learning curve into a matter for sociological study. And surely these technological divides add yet another layer to the already wide global disparities. To follow these patterns of global disparities, technological and other, let me start by considering the way we gauge technology on a global scale. It is through this discussion of measurement that we identify trends and tendencies.

Measuring the World by Technology: ICT as a Scale of Achievement

Nations account for their ICT accomplishments proudly: they report on it in government documents and in public announcements. Some stress their technological status vis-à-vis other nations to emphasize the relative status of their accomplishments. To make such cross-national comparisons possible, governments and various agencies rely on the work of international organizations whose primary interest is the field of ICT. Such international organizations as the United Nations Development Programme (UNDP), the United Nations Education, Science, and Cultural Organization (UNESCO), and the International Telecommunication Union (ITU) not only gather and compile comparative information about national technological achievements, thus allowing points of comparison, but they also rank countries by their achievement in the field and single out the leaders.

Such a celebration of technological success was offered in the UNDP's *Human Development Report* of 2001. The report was devoted solely to technological achievement: it celebrated the role of technology in delivering human prosperity and pointed to technology as a necessity for any future prospects of progress. Specifically, the report concentrated on two sorts of technologies: information and communication technology and biomedicine. UNDP went to great lengths to offer a picture of the worldwide conditions and trends of these technologies, thus compiling rich data on various technological features. To complement its data compilation work,

UNDP also ranked countries by their technological achievement. Both these goals—data gathering and ranking of countries—are important to my discussion of the global digital divide, in spite of their appearance as a straightforward matter of organizational strategy; therefore, let me elaborate on them further.

First, UNDP compiled information on various dimensions of technology, aggregated into the national level, and indexed them in the Technology Achievement Index (TAI). TAI offers a single value score per nation on a scale of 0–1. Ordered by their TAI score, nations were ranked (1 through 72) and also grouped into five categories by technological achievement: leaders, potential leaders, dynamic adopters, marginalized, and others. The measurement and calculation of TAI and the grouping of countries that arises from it may seem a technical matter; it is, however, a political process of defining what is considered "technology," which technology is "high" or "low," which technology-related activities are regarded as "modern" and "useful."

Specifically, the eight components of the index identify various dimensions of technology:

◆ Technology creation: Measured by both patents granted to residents and receipts of royalties and license fees
◆ Diffusion of recent technologies: Measured by Internet hosts and high- and medium-technology exports
◆ Diffusion of old innovations: Measured by telephones and electricity consumption
◆ Human skills, implying the potential of future technology creation: Measured by years of schooling for adults and science enrollments in tertiary education

The focus on these technology-related measures rather than on others symbolizes the model of desirable and rewarded technology by current global values. These measures reflect a celebration of creativity and innovation (rather than utilization and adaptation), of new and fashionable technologies (rather than technologies that are useful to most of humanity), and of the human capital of workers. UNDP thus fails in spite of its best efforts to broaden the definition of technology: its measures reflect a focus solely on high tech. For example, the "old technologies" for which UNDP compiles cross-national data and which it includes in the calculation of TAI are telephones and electricity consumption. These are basically infrastructural technologies for advanced ICT; they do not reflect the sorts of "old" technologies that are useful for the upgrading of living conditions for most of humanity, such as water pumps, tractors, and cars. Similarly, when considering "human skills," UNDP focuses on advanced education and training, namely the level of schooling of people age 15 and above and the ratio of population in tertiary education. However, most countries are still struggling to achieve universal literacy and adequate elementary and secondary education. This gap between expectations and actual capacity is made clearer when comparing achievement for each type of technology: when comparing technology achievement scores on high tech versus low tech, it is clear that greater inequality is evident when advanced and newer technology is considered.

Similarly, the premium given to innovation and creativity is reflected in the rank order and grouping of nations. The groups labeled as "leaders," "potential leaders," and "dynamic adapters" are differentiated by their ability to create new technology. This is evident because the clearest demarcation among nations is on the scale of technology creation and only to a lesser degree on the scales of the diffusion of recent innovations, the diffusion of old innovations, or even human skills. This reflects more than a gap in the ability to innovate (what is referred to as the "innovation gap" and discussed at length in Chapter 4); it is a normative bonus given to discovery, expansion, imagination, and ingenuity. All these are also core elements of the "pioneer spirit" that is so endemic to modern scientific discourse, most pronounced in the legacy of Vannevar Bush and his ideals of science as the endless (and new) frontier. Bush, who founded the U.S. military's research wing and later the National Science Foundation (among other private and public R&D-intensive organizations), was not only instrumental to the development of the computer, but he also served as the prime visionary for the computer age. His 1945 report to President Roosevelt, titled "Science: The Endless Frontier," codified the vision of science as the positive force in progress: science is the source for public welfare, as well as for wartime defense and peacetime prosperity and health. The report begins with these strong words:

> Scientific Progress is Essential. Progress in the war against disease depends upon a flow of new scientific knowledge. New products, new industries, and more jobs require continuous additions to knowledge of the laws of nature, and the application of that knowledge to practical purposes. Similarly, our defense against aggression demands new knowledge so that we can develop new and improved weapons. This essential, new knowledge can be obtained only through basic scientific research.

> Science can be effective in the national welfare only as a member of a team, whether the conditions be peace or war. But without scientific progress no amount of achievement in other directions can insure our health, prosperity, and security as a nation in the modern world.[31]

This Bush spirit influences the planning of scientific and R&D endeavors today. UNDP's ranking and rewarding of countries on the TAI scale is a clear example of the vision that scientific achievement equals progress. Those falling behind in science and technology are, then, underdeveloped and lagging in progress. On the TAI scale, the obvious cases are yet again marginalized and labeled as laggers, or deviants, when it comes to economic development and human progress. The countries in the last two groups in UNDP's ranking by TAI are labeled "marginalized" and "others." Clearly, these countries are lagging behind on almost all measures of ICT. Yet they are not lagging on all measures. Senegal, which is ranked as a marginalized country, reports 28.5% of its total goods exports in 1999 to be high- and medium-technology goods, while in Norway and New Zealand (both grouped among the world leaders) such shares are at 19% and 15.4%, respectively. What the countries in the category "marginalized" clearly share, then, is a lack of data on technology creation or on ability to innovate. For these failings, they are penalized and labeled as "marginalized."[32]

In addition to indexing technology achievement and grouping countries into "categories of distance," UNDP also uses the idea of global technology hubs to celebrate and reward innovation (Box 2.1). On a geographical map of the world, particular centers of innovation are highlighted; they are also identified by the magnitude of innovation in each one.[33] UNDP identified 46 centers of innovation: from Silicon Valley in California and Route 128 outside Boston to El Ghazala in Tunisia and Gautend in South Africa. Although there is often some correspondence between the TAI rank of a country and the number of technology hubs within its borders,[34] this is not always the case: for example, Brazil is classified as merely a "dynamic adopter" though it has two local-yet-global technology hubs on its soil (Sao Paulo and Campinas), while Argentina is classified as a "potential leader" but has no hub to pride itself on. The identification of technology hubs, specifically defined as "locations that matter most in the new digital geography,"[35] is a celebration of the "big winners": technology hubs are emblematic and unique badges of honor and pride in technological achievement, over and above TAI scores.

The celebration of technological success is, then, a reward for "winners"; the "losers" are left behind, trailing in the ranking of access to and utilization of the distinguished new technology. The "losers" become a nonstory: their tale is not one to be learned and emulated by other nations. Yet the tale of the "losers" is very revealing: it allows us a window into an alternative scale of world technology, namely a scale of technological *under*achievement.

Box 2.1

Where Are the Global Technology Hubs?

In the August 2000 issue of *Wired* magazine, Jennifer Hillner identified 46 global technological hubs as the centers of the new digital economy. These hubs are defined as the geographical locations that are most important to the new era of digital technology. Their importance is determined by four dimensions of digital technoeconomic activity: (a) the capacity of area institutions of higher education to train skilled personnel in the technical fields and to develop new technologies, (b) the presence of established companies and multinational corporations in the area, (c) the entrepreneurial spirit of the local population, and (d) the availability of venture capital to sponsor the transition of technology into the market. As a technical means of determining such importance, global sites were ranked on a scale of 1–4 on each such dimension, and the total score (ranging between 0 and 16) was calculated. This ranking, based on interviews with industry leaders and technology analysts, identified a total of 46 global technology hubs, titled by Hillner "venture capitals":

Silicon Valley, USA (16)
Boston, USA (15)
Stockholm-Kista, Sweden (15)
Israel (15)
Raleigh-Durham-Chapel Hill,
 USA (14)
London, UK (14)
Helsinki, Finland (14)
Austin, USA (13)
San Francisco, USA (13)
Taipei, Taiwan (13)
Bangalore, India (13)
New York City, USA (12)
Albuquerque, USA (12)
Montreal, Canada (12)
Seattle, USA (12)
Cambridge, UK (12)
Dublin, Ireland (12)
Los Angeles, USA (11)
Malmo, Sweden/Copenhagen,
 Denmark (11)
Bavaria, Germany (11)
Flanders, Belgium (11)
Tokyo, Japan (11)

Kyoto, Japan (11)
Hsinchu, Taiwan (11)
Virginia, USA (10)
Thames Valley, UK (10)
Paris, France (10)
Baden-Wurtemberg, Germany (10)
Oulu, Finland (10)
Melbourne, Australia (10)
Chicago, USA (9)
Hong Kong, China (9)
Queensland, Australia (9)
Sao Paulo, Brazil (9)
Salt Lake City, USA (8)
Santa Fe, USA (8)
Glasgow-Edinburgh, UK (8)
Saxony, Germany (8)
Sophia Antipolis, France (8)
Inchon, South Korea (8)
Kuala Lumpur, Malaysia (8)
Campinas, Brazil (8)
Singapore (7)
Trondheim, Norway (6)
El Ghazala, Tunisia (4)
Gauteng, South Africa (4)

A few issues regarding this delineation of global technology hubs are important to note. First, all locations, except for the small nations of Israel and Singapore, are cities or provinces within nations, highlighting the geographical concentration of high-tech industries even when they are dispersed across the globe. This geographical concentration points up the within-nation inequalities in access to new technology. Some nations are marked as global technology leaders, but it is actually particular regions within them that carry the "badge of honor" while other provinces and cities lag technologically and look more like the marginalized nations of the world. This is how global inequalities, here technology-related, are layered: regional development is then layered on national ranking, which is layered yet further by such social markers as race, gender, and nationality. In this sense, the scaling of global centrality/marginality as is portrayed in this identification of regional rankings is only the tip of the iceberg.

Second, while almost all countries identified by UNDP 2001 as "technology leaders" have at least one tech hub in their territory (the United States has 13), more technology hubs exist in countries that are identified in the category "dynamic adopters" (ranked third) than in the category of "potential leaders" (ranked second). This means that the global spatial arrangement of technology hubs has two "heads"—in the highly advanced nations and in the semiperipheral, tech-aspiring nations—whereas the intermediate group of "potential leaders" does not have such established centers of high tech. These issues converge at a general point: having a tech hub within a country does not necessarily mean that the country, as a whole, is more technologically savvy.

Last, Hillner's label of these locales as "venture capitals" sharpens the definition of power and centrality in the new economy as resting on the combination of entrepreneurship (in terms of both capital and innovation) and technology (in terms of the focus of such sponsorship). This neoliberal economic tone of global stratification rankings is an issue discussed throughout this book.

Measuring from the Bottom Up: E-Waste Sites as the Indication of Technological *Under*achievement

Consumption and utilization of technology, including new technology, create huge and ever-growing capacity problems,[36] the most acute of which currently is the problem of e-waste. Hazardous electronic waste, or e-waste, refers to computer products: old PCs and their components, as well as wires and networking equipment. The problem is not merely the physical space that such disposal requires, as is the case when decomposed waste is considered; rather, computer components are laced with toxic materials[37] that threaten the health of people and their environment for years to come.

How big is this problem? It is huge. What is championed as the expansion of the high-tech sector and the technological upgrading of governments and businesses means a rapid turnover of technological tools: a rapid replacement of old devices with new ones. It is estimated that during the 1990s the lifespan of a computer had shrunk from five years to only two. The National Safety Council's Environmental Health Center projected in 1999 that in the United States alone 500 million PC systems would become obsolete between 1997 and 2007 and that only 14% of American PCs are recycled or reconditioned.[38] So where is this e-waste disposed of? Mostly in developing countries and in rural America: in the margins of global society.

Recycling of hazardous electronic waste is regulated: the Basel Convention of 1992 (Box 2.2) regulates traffic in hazardous waste and bans the exports of hazardous materials from industrial to nonindustrial countries. But although only three countries, namely Afghanistan, Haiti, and the United States, have not yet ratified the Basel Convention, plenty of others are violating its rules already. As a report titled "Export Harm: The High Tech Trashing of Asia" recounts, any export of e-waste to countries that do not have adequate environmental regulation and enforcement is not "recycling" but rather "e-dumping." There exists a strong incentive to "recycle" hazardous e-waste in developing nations rather than within one's own boundaries: according to 1988 estimates, it cost up to US$2,500 per ton to dispose of highly toxic waste in the United States mainly because of the overhead costs of disposal and policing. At that time, this waste could be disposed of in some developing countries for as little as US$3 per ton.[39] These cost considerations encourage global corporations to put the pressure on developing countries; they also set the global hierarchy of economic dumping.

When the technology-related global hierarchy is considered, the comparison of e-dumping with the ranking of TAI is telling. The most common e-dumping sites are in Pakistan, India, and China. These three countries, high in the ranking of e-dumping, are at the bottom of the Technology Achievement Index: China is 45, India 63, and Pakistan 65 (in a 72-country list). In this sense, becoming a site for e-dumping is an indicator of technological *under*achievement, or the inverse of technological achievement. These sites of e-dumping in developing areas mark the margins of the ICT world. As illustrated in the following tale of a worker in a Chinese town that became a site for global e-dumping, technological achievement mixes with underachievement: big corporate names of the global ICT sector appear side-by-side with signs of extreme poverty. The margins of the ICT world are also marked by other dimensions of social exclusion: illness, meager income, and lack of access to clear water.

Box 2.2

The Basel Convention

The Basel Convention, formally titled the Basel Convention on the Control of Transboundary Movements of Hazardous Wastes and Their Disposal, was finalized in an international conference on the subject in Basel, Switzerland, on March 22, 1989. The convention was drafted in response to increasing concerns about the international trafficking of hazardous waste. Since the 1980s the accumulation of evidence about the massive expansion in the quantities of hazardous waste, made dramatic by a few front-page scandalous affairs of bribery of high officials in developing countries to accept hazardous waste, increased international pressure to regulate the disposal of the waste and to bridge the North–South divide in the generation and clearance of such waste.

Emerging from international negotiations that started in 1987, the Basel Convention took effect on May 5, 1992 (amendments were made in 1998), and compliance with its rules is currently monitored by its secretariat (administered by the United Nations Environment Programme). A total of 155 countries ratified the convention, with Afghanistan, Haiti, and the United States maintaining only signatory commitment to it. The convention regulates trafficking and disposal of hazardous waste, defined as "toxic, poisonous, explosive, corrosive, flammable, ecotoxic and infectious" waste, which includes almost all components of digital technology (especially cellular phones and computers).

The convention is guided by three basic principles. First, in response to estimates that some 300 to 500 million tons of hazardous waste are generated annually,* the convention calls for the creation of hazardous waste to be minimized. Second, since 90% of the world's hazardous waste is generated in the *developed* world[†] and since most of it is disposed of in the *developing* world, the convention calls for hazardous waste to be treated and disposed of as close as possible to its source of generation to correct this global imbalance, not to say exploitation. Last, the convention calls for establishing sound environmental regulations in countries worldwide to shore up local safeguards against exploitation and to ensure recourse in case of violations. As preventive measures, the Basel protocol calls also for promotion of cleaner and safer technologies and for the dissemination of information about the dangers of hazardous waste and about recommended "environmentally sound management" of development. For more information, see http://www.unep.ch/basel/ (accessed March 27, 2003). See also commentary of international non-governmental organizations on the Basel Convention, specifically by The Basel Action Network (BAN) http://www.ban.org/ (accessed March 27, 2003).

---

*Katherine Kummer (1995), *International Management of Hazardous Wastes: The Basel Convention and Related Legal Rules* (Oxford: Clarendon Press).

[†]Marian A. L. Miller (1995), *The Third World in Global Environmental Politics* (Boulder, CO: Lynne Reinner).

Before farmer Tai Chunhua walked away from the fields of China's Jiangxi Province and headed south for Guiyu town in Guangdong, he hadn't seen a computer in his 21 years. Three years later his working day sees him surrounded by the hi-tech gadgetry of Dell, Hewlett Packard, IBM, Toshiba, Hitachi, Apple, Compaq, Epson, Xerox . . . the issue of just about every big-name manufacturer of electronic office equipment on the planet.

Dressed in a black cotton shirt, healthily tanned and with neatly cut hair, Tai is a specialist in the office equipment game. His field of expertise is toner cartridges for printers and photocopier machines. He doesn't design the cartridges. He doesn't sell them or even install them. He smashes them into bits to salvage the tiny amounts of residual toner. For this dirty, polluting task he might make RMB 20 (HK $18) a day. For his troubles he might also be rewarded with respiratory and skin disease, eye infections, even cancer. [. . .]

Every year Guiyu takes in more than a million tons of computer waste, earning its residents, according to mainland press reports, RMB 1 billion. All day, every day, mountains of wire and other equipment are burned in Guiyu streets to obtain copper and other scrap metals. Printed circuit boards are heated over charcoal burners to liberate them of computer chips that might be reusable. The boards are then soaked in acid to extract gold, and the waste dumped alongside or in the nearby Lianjiang River. Printer cartridges are ripped apart for their toner and recyclable aluminum, steel and plastic parts. Cathode-ray tubes are hammered open for their copper yokes.

The result is that the air, land, and water on which local people depend have all been poisoned. Local well water is already undrinkable, even after boiling, and fresh supplies must be trucked in from the town of Chan Dim 15 kilometers away. [. . .]

Poverty forced Tai down the pollution road. "Life in Jiangxi is very poor, there isn't much work to do," he says. "My family is poor, we don't have money—if we did I wouldn't have come here." He tries to make light of his toil. On opening a cartridge, the dark powder flutters up to his face. "It is minor matter, no problem," he says with a quick laugh.[40]

The town of Guiyu, unknown to most computer users, marks the final station for globally celebrated computer technology. Guiyu is, then, linked to the global industry and community of ICT, while also marginalized by it. In this, Guiyu joins many other small, anonymous towns in developing areas in a network of e-dumping sites. It is in such locales in Asia that 85% of American "recycled" PCs end up. This amount of American e-waste will probably only increase, once additional American states join California and Massachusetts in banning the disposal of cathode ray tubes (CRTs) in local landfills. Moreover, California and Massachusetts are now used as models for the United States Environmental Protection Agency's (EPA) proposed regulation to ban all CRTs and mercury-containing waste from American landfills. Although this regulation (proposed in September 2002) will relieve the toxic pressure on rural and marginalized regions in the United States, it will push all e-waste toward the global margins: towns like Guiyu in China's Guangdong Province or Dobbespet, some 50 kilometers outside

Bangalore, India. The more pressure mounts in developing countries (from tight regulatory regimes and a conscientious public), the more it becomes lucrative to release this pressure on developing countries where environmental sensitivities are weak and labor costs are low.[41] With this, says the Basel Action Network (BAN), the American EPA is perpetuating a policy of global environmental injustice. Global injustice equals global inequality.

Increasingly, developing countries add to their own misery. With rising incomes to allow consumption of digital technology and with information society initiatives to bring computers to all, developing countries are now contributing to the mounting e-waste. India alone produced e-waste worth US$1.5 billion during 2003. India is expected to see 2 million personal computers below the Pentium 1 grade junked within the three years 2004–2007; the 1,150 information technology companies near Bangalore alone generate 6,000 tons of lethal electronic waste annually. "It is a myth that e-waste can be fully recycled," states a report by the Indian nongovernmental environmental protection organization Toxics Links.[42]

Although few dispute the trend of global technological inequality, debates still rage over the magnitude and trajectory of the global digital divide. First, while no one is challenging the notion that great disparity in use and capacity of digital technology exists across the world, it is still not clear to all what the trends of technological diffusion are. Are we seeing a divergence or convergence among countries and among populations around the world? Proponents of the "normalization thesis" claim that even existing disparities are not a major cause for concern because all social resources (other than capital) tend to be more equally distributed over time.[43] Second, it is a matter of debate whether the trends of diffusion of digital technology are similar across the specific technologies. There are hints that some technologies diffuse faster than others (Internet use has a faster global diffusion rate than PC ownership) and that some differential diffusion is geopolitically specific (cellular phone use is growing more rapidly in semiperipheral countries than in the rich core or in the poor developing sectors). Third, the position of the United States as the absolute world leader in ICT achievement dampens the prospects of a catch-up strategy, especially for developing countries that lag far behind on all dimensions of the global digital divide. To evaluate the various stands on these debates, we must understand the depth of the phenomenon of the global digital divide. By mapping the social and global conditions of technological diffusion and by identifying the patterns for its differential rates of technology, we are able to describe the social features, or characteristics, that segment, if not explain, such trends.

Notes

1. Jeffrey Sachs (2000, June 24). "A New Map of the World." *Economist*.
2. Benjamin M. Compaine (ed.) (2001), *The Digital Divide: Facing a Crisis or Creating a Myth?* (Cambridge, MA: MIT Press), p. 325.
3. International Telecommunication Union (2003), *World Telecommunication Development Report: Summary* (Geneva: ITU, World Summit on the Information Society), p. 5.
4. World Bank (2004), *2004 Development Indicators* (Washington, DC: World Bank), p. 296.
5. Linda Main (2001), "The Global Information Infrasturcture: Empowerment or Imperialism?" *Third World Development* 22(1): 83–97.
6. United Nations Development Programme (2004), *Human Development Report 2004: Cultural Liberty in Today's Diverse World* (Washington, DC: UNDP), p. 183.
7. Amanda Lenhart, John Horrigan, Lee Rainie, Katherine Allen, Angie Boyce, Mary Madden, and Erin O'Grach (2003), *The Ever-Shifting Internet Population: A New Look at Internet Access and the Digital Divide* (Washington DC: Pew Internet and American Life Project).
8. United Nations Development Programme (2001), *Human Development Report 2001: Making New Technologies Work for Human Development* (New York: UNDP), pp. 2, 33.
9. Comprising both ISP price (the fee collected by the Internet service provider for access through its service) and phone charges (for accessing the ISP).
10. International Telecommunication Union (2001), *Numbering Cyberspace: Recent Trends in the Internet World* (Telecommunication Indicators Update, January/February/March 2001), http://www.itu.int/ITU-D/ict/statistics, accessed October 31, 2002.
11. UNDP (2001), note 8, p. 5.
12. UNDP (2001), note 8, p. 3.
13. This figure of speech, portraying the "escape" of potential users in spite of the increasing density of this communication network and its reaches, has been used repeatedly to describe the failure of the digital revolution to reach the general population. It became prevalent after being offered as the title of a series of reports by the U.S. National Telecommunications and Information Administration. The 1995 report was titled "Falling through the Net: A Survey of the 'Have-Nots' in Rural and Urban America," and the 1999 report was titled "Falling through the Net: Defining the Digital Divide."
14. ITU (2001), note 10, p. 1.

15. UNDP (2001), note 8, p. 3.
16. UNDP (2001), note 8, p. 39.
17. UNDP (2001), note 8, pp. 3, 9.
18. UNDP (2001), note 8, p. 39.
19. UNDP (2001), note 8, p. 40.
20. Pipa Norris, W. Lance Bennett, and Robert M. Entman (2001), *Digital Divide: Civic Engagement, Information Poverty, and the Internet Worldwide* (Cambridge, UK: Cambridge University Press), p. 45.
21. UNDP (2001), note 8, p. 3.
22. UNDP (2001), note 8, p. 42.
23. UNDP (2001), note 8, p. 48.
24. ITU (2001), note 10, p. 3.
25. Nua Internet Surveys 2000 data in Norris et al., note 20, p. 47.
26. UNDP (2001), note 8, p. 3.
27. Main (2001), note 5, p. 94.
28. UNDP (2001), note 8, pp. 80–81.
29. UNDP (2001), note 8, p. 144.
30. World Bank (2000), *World Development Indicators,* CD-ROM and http://www.worldbank.org/data/wdi/index.htm.
31. Vannevar Bush (1945, July), "Science: The Endless Frontier," report to President Franklin D. Roosevelt (Washington, DC: U.S. Government Printing Office).
32. They are not only relegated to the "marginalized" category; they are specifically assigned to the group labeled "others." Most of these countries are missing data on most indicators, which hints at a total absence of infrastructure, even to monitor and report science and technology activity.
33. See UNDP (2001), note 8, p. 45.
34. For example, the United States, which leads the world by far when it comes to high tech, has 13 (out of 46) technology hubs in its territory.
35. UNDP (2001), note 8, p. 45.
36. One capacity problem is the overload of the electricity and telephone systems for the ever-growing demand for power supply and networking capacity.
37. The most prevalent toxic material is lead, a critical component in the coating of cathode ray tubes (CRTs) that are used to light up computer and TV screens. The lead, while not endangering computer users, is released into the environment when the tubes are cracked or opened. It then becomes highly toxic to workers handling e-waste, and it seeps into the soil to pollute underground reservoirs.
38. Henry Norr (2001, May 27), "Drowning in e-Waste: Safe Disposal of Mountains of Old PCs, Monitors Is a Snowballing Problem We've Only Begun to Face," *San Francisco Chronicle.*

39. Marian A. L. Miller (1995), *The Third World in Global Environmental Politics* (Boulder, CO: Lynne Reinner), p. 88.

40. Excerpts from Sherry Lee (2002, May 12), "Ghosts in the Machines," *South China Morning Post Magazine,* available on http://www.ban.org/Library/ghosts_in.html, accessed October 31, 2002.

41. For more on the pressure on developing countries to accept electronic waste and the damage to their environments, see M. Raja (2004, April 6), "E-Wasting Away in India," *Asia Times Online,* http://www.atimes.com/atimes/South_Asia/FD06Df02.html, accessed April 26, 2004.

42. Quoted in Raja (2004), note 41.

43. See Chapters 3 and 4 for additional discussions of the "normalization thesis."

A Matter of Access and Use

The Social Features of the Global Digital Divide

Global inequality is crystallized in differential access to social resources; in our discussions here, we refer specifically to the social resource of digital technology. Differential access to technology means that not all people have equal, undisturbed, and unbiased ability to reach the technology. Some people can more easily access and use technology than others. The fortunate ones have the personal wealth to purchase a PC, live in communities that offer Internet use in public libraries or government offices, and acquire the skills to use these technologies as a part of their basic education. Others, the marginalized citizens of this global village, lack all access to and use of digital technology. They live in areas that lack the infrastructure for the use of digital technology (no electricity, telephone connection, or cellular networks); they lack the skills to use digital technology (because they are illiterate or have no basic familiarity with computers); they lack both the personal funds and the access to social services to acquire either the technology or the skills. Similarly, these factors contribute to a gap in use of the technology: differential use of technology means that not all people have equal, undisturbed, and unbiased ability to utilize the technology.

Together, access to and use of technology serve as the features of the digital divide, across nations and within them. The digital divide has, then, multiple dimensions: physical access (can I locate a PC to sit in front of?), financial access (can I afford the cost of purchasing a PC and paying the access fees?), cognitive access (am I interested in logging on and do I understand the impact it may have on my life?), content access (do I understand what is available to me through digital technology and can I understand the language in which the information is offered?), and political access (does my government allow me to access the full range of available information?).[1] Even if such barriers are overcome and digital technology is accessible and available, other barriers exist to prohibit full use of digital technology: users may be illiterate or not speak the language in which software is written; they may be under social pressure not to use digital technology; they may be restricted by censorship laws. Access and use are, therefore, distinct issues. "Access" describes the availability of the technology; "use" refers to utilization of the technology once it is available. Moreover, the digital divide is composed of divides between states, between communities, and between individuals, which intersect with the dimensions of access and use.

As shown before in statistical breakdowns by national income and geopolitical location, differential access to digital technology is not accidental or random. Rather, it follows the contours of social demarcation. Barriers to free access are systematic, rewarding groups of individuals unevenly and preventing equal or proportional shares of access to social resources. These groups, often referred to as "minorities," are classified by such criteria of social worthiness as gender, ethnicity, nationality, race, religion, and age. Although in principle most societies claim these criteria to be irrelevant for social rewards and inconsequential for social status, these traditional and persistent notions of worthiness are unfortunately perpetuating social divides and are now applied to discriminatory access to new social resources, such as digital technology.

One model conceptualizing the problem of discriminatory access to and use of social resources is the "pipeline model." This common understanding describes society as an input/output system in which people are streamlined through a sequence of pipes and channels. Each section of the pipe delivers its human output to the next and thus enables a continuous flow. This model describes in particular education and career tracks: the input into the system is children who are entering schools; the schools teach them the relevant skills and social values; the schools deliver them as output into the workforce. This "supply side" image of social access and of the utilization of human capital is very explicit and inspired the cover of a 1992 issue of *Science* magazine that included a discussion of "leaks" in the pipeline. "Leaks" are any dropouts in the system of delivery, from school attrition and failure to make the grade to the mismatch of skills acquired to a job. But are there "weak joints" in the pipeline that are more

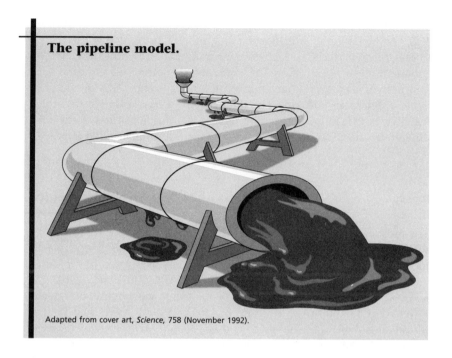

The pipeline model.

Adapted from cover art, *Science*, 758 (November 1992).

prone to leaks? And if so, are these "weak joints" systematic, having some particular nature? Although the pipeline model is clearly important in revealing social barriers (leaks) to understanding problems of development (output), it focuses solely on the failure.

Still, what about the failure of the "pipeline" to deliver its output? Are the "leaks" patterned and group-based? Or are social inequalities categorical? Charles Tilly, in his 1999 book *Durable Inequalities*, stresses that human inequalities may not be understood if conceptualized as gradational: economists and other professional groups emphasizing "methodological individualism" see inequality in terms of income distribution, often charted as a sequence of rewards for skills.[2] The perception of inequality as gradational represents inequality as a sequence of continuous dimensions stretching unbroken between poor and rich that masks the crucial role of categorical differentiation: men/woman, black/white, citizen/non-citizen, and others. These categories mark a person and classify his or her life chances. They are important as first impressions and also dramatize group differences in access to resources.

I, like Tilly, take issue with these expressions of "methodological individualism." True, some such categories are not dichotomous: race and

ethnicity are multicategorical, especially in today's open-border countries. Still, the hierarchy of worthiness and appropriateness among these scales of categorical markers is clear: whites earn more then all other racial groups, suburban dwellers earn more than residents of both cities and rural areas, and natives earn more than immigrants or transients. This is true of income differentials and longevity differentials; it is also true of technological divides. The following sections identify the group features along which differences in ICT access and diffusion are most dramatically patterned.

The Income Divide

The most apparent difference in access to digital technology is income, or wealth: poor people utilize digital technology less than do rich people. Evidence about this income gap is consistent across countries. In the United States in 2000, 60% of Americans with household income greater than $35,000 were on-line, while only 42% of people with household income lower than $35,000 were on-line;[3] in Japan in 2001 more than half the households with income greater than 8 million yen (equivalent to US$70,000) or higher were on-line, while only one quarter of the households with income of less than 4 million yen (equivalent to US$35,000) were on-line; in South Korea in 2001, 70% of Koreans whose monthly incomes were greater than 2.5 million won (equivalent to US$2,000) were on-line, while only 37% of Koreans with a monthly income smaller than 1.5 million won (equivalent to US$1,250) were on-line. With a few exceptions, then, a person's income is a strong predictor of use of digital technology. The exceptions are telling, too. One such exception is in the type of digital technology used: in Japan, because mobile phones are widely used as a gateway to the Internet (more so than PCs) and because use of mobile phones is very popular, mobile phone–based Internet access is more evenly distributed across social groups than access through PCs. The second exception in the impact of income on the digital divide is related to the availability of public access: in China, for example, 17% of those with no income are still Internet users. This does not necessarily mean that in China even the poor have access to the Internet; those recorded as having no income are students, who can log on in public access sites such as their universities or schools. Another case of public access occurs in South Korea. Although Korea is a world leader in broadband Internet access— high-speed and high-capacity access is available throughout the land—the income divide in access and use of digital technology has actually widened since 1999. Public access has not bridged the digital gaps; rather, the income divide still reinforces the digital divide.

As is the case between income categories of individuals, so is the digital divide evident between income categories of nations: poor countries have a smaller share of access to digital technology than do rich countries. Some aspects of this global cross-national income divide were described earlier. When categorizing countries by their income level, we clearly see that although Internet use and PC ownership are expanding in all three groups of countries, the dramatic expansion occurs in affluent countries (see Figures 2.1 and 2.2). In this sense, even though middle-income and low-income countries are rapidly increasing their use of digital media, their share of this media sector still falls far short of their worldwide population share: their catch-up rate is impressive mostly because the starting point was so low.

As mentioned in Chapter 2, though great variety exists within each income category, even within the category of developed and affluent nations, there is a dramatic digital gap among countries. Members of the Organisation for Economic Co-operation and Development (OECD) differ greatly on the number of Internet hosts per 1,000 people, as well as on the differentials in Internet dial-up costs. Similar gaps exist among the still smaller group of European nations: in 1999, ten times as many people were on-line in Sweden as in Portugal and Greece, and tour times as many Swedes as Greeks owned PCs. These differences reveal a dramatic variation in digital capacity and access even in the exclusive group of economically advanced and technologically sophisticated countries.

Still, the United States dominates the digital world and leads all other countries by a huge margin. As mentioned in the previous chapter, the United States outcompetes even other Western nations in the rate of Internet penetration. These differences among Western countries yet again highlight the distinction between relative and absolute Internet capacity. Per capita ratios and growth rates in Internet access are high in all Western countries, indicating a solid base of use and a rapid rate of change in digital capacity access across the West, yet the United States remains the distant leader because of its overwhelming, absolute dominance of the Internet field. In this sense, the rapid expansion of the Internet may give the impression that Internet laggers are catching up to the leaders at an astounding rate, yet currently the United States is still by far the global leader in Internet capacity and use. In addition, the catch-up rate of digital laggers differs by type of technology, and this difference is most relevant in technologies that require an infrastructure, specifically, telephones: digital cellular phones permit users to communicate even in the absence of land-line infrastructure. As a result, we see the highest rate of expansion in the use of mobile phones in high-income non-OECD countries to bypass the infrastructure problem of the absence of a solid and expansive land-line telephone system.

The income divide is true of digital technology and new media; it is true also of old media. Norris, Bennett, and Entman show that low-income countries, which have by far lower percentages of on-line population, Internet hosts, PCs, and cellular phones, also have much lower ratios of access to radios, TVs, daily newspapers, and land-line phones.[4] Moreover, countries that have an established base of old media use are more likely to use new, or digital, media. Hence, differential access to information, through whatever media, is lower in poor countries than in richer ones.

In this sense, even involvement in the global ICT industrial sector is not a reflection of better access: vertical integration of various nations and world regions into the ICT manufacturing and consumption networks marks a division of labor and "locks" the countries into a rigid sector structure. The global division of labor, then, parallels income divides, making use of cheap labor costs and high human capital skills in middle-income countries such as India and Taiwan. A. T. Kearney, calculating an index of country attractiveness for off-shore IT outsourcing, highlights India in particular and also Canada, Brazil, and Mexico as leading the list: in these countries the higher education system supplies highly trained IT professionals, the financial and business sectors are on a par with Western standards, and the costs of labor and land are low.[5] And, with the means of ICT, IT companies are able to work around the clock, dividing tasks among their various locales: the same task is allocated for eight-hour shifts among three locales, divided by the GMT, so the same task is worked on continuously. In an era that requires rapid progress and quick new-generation product development, this global division of labor expedites the R&D process. Some such division of labor is implied in the categorization of the Technology Achievement Index (TAI). Some countries are innovators and leaders in the global technology field, others are manufacturers and adaptors of technology (thus followers), and yet others are sites of e-dumping (thus laggers). All such tasks—from development and manufacturing to dumping—are associated with the country's income capacity.

The Regional Divide

Global digital inequality also follows the boundaries of regional location. Clearly, North American countries (the United States and Canada) and Scandinavian countries (Sweden, Norway, Finland, Iceland, and Denmark) cluster into the most developed ICT regions. These seven countries lead the world in the percent of population on-line (in all, it is higher than 50%) and they alone account for some 50% of the worldwide share of on-line population. Their lead over all other regions is across the ICT board:

in costs of hardware and connection, in use of various digital media, in digital infrastructure (like bandwidth and cellular zones), and in leading the future of ICT in R&D and in venture capital investments in ICT. These regions were the early adopters of digital technology and they are the leaders in its use and development today.

On the opposite side of this regional distinction stands Africa.[6] In 2000, the average on-line population in 52 African countries was only 0.5%; African countries also dramatically lag in terms of the local availability of Internet hosts, mobile phones, and PCs. So although sub-Saharan Africa accounts for about one sixth of the world's population, it is home to only 1% of the world's on-line community. The number of Internet hosts throughout sub-Saharan Africa is smaller than the number of hosts in New York City alone; the number of Internet hosts in the whole of Latin America and the Caribbean equals the number of hosts in France alone.

Still, why should geography matter in an age of transnationality and global communications? Why should geographical proximity determine the condition and trajectory of ICT use? Indeed, ICT has enabled greater geographical dispersion of the IT sector and its popular use across the globe. As mentioned earlier, around-the-clock production links a network of R&D sites that are in different locales, and e-mail exchanges link academic institutions across the globe. Maybe, then, geography is only a proxy for other global divides: North American countries are also wealthy and English-speaking and Scandinavian countries are democratic welfare states that offer a wide range of social services to their citizens, while African countries are the poorest and least educated, plagued with corrupt regimes and torn apart by civil strife.

As a sociologist I prefer, then, to see global divides, especially divides in digital technology capacity, not in terms of geographical locations and natural resources, but rather in social terms: political and economic conditions, social definitions of roles and preferences, and social resources of education and language. The markers of the global digital divide are related to endemic problems of development and social disenfranchisement: they are marked by racial affiliation and patterns of leisure time use, occupation, and literacy. The following sections describe the global digital divide in such sociological terms.

The Gender Divide

The most pronounced social difference in access to and use of digital technology is along gender lines: women, by far and across the world, constitute a smaller share of users of digital technology (Figure 3.1). The numbers

Figure 3.1

Proportion of Female Internet Users by Country, 2000 (% of total)

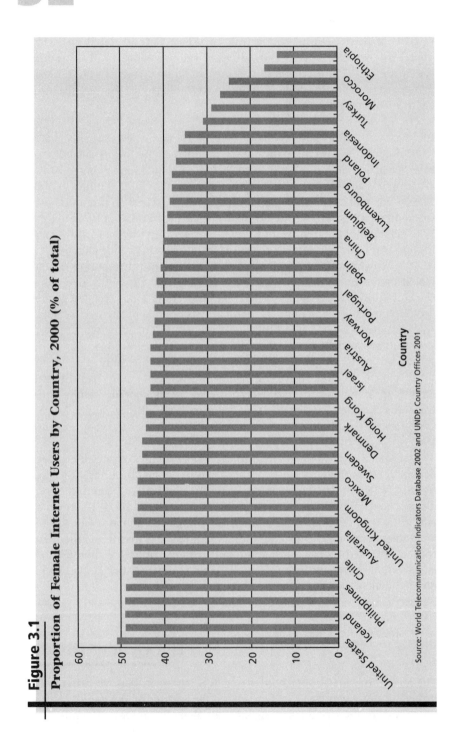

Source: World Telecommunication Indicators Database 2002 and UNDP, Country Offices 2001

are rather astonishing: in China, only 30% of Internet users are female; in Ethiopia and Senegal women's share of Internet users is 14% and 17%, respectively; in the Arab world women account for only 4% of the local on-line population. In a 1999 survey of women in two Kenyan provinces, 99% of women had never heard of e-mail.[7]

Data on women's use of digital technology is sketchy; I suspect that the interest in women as a distinct category of technology users is a recent phenomenon, related to the definition of the global digital divide as a social problem and to feminist critiques of technology, and thus data have been collected only recently. Data are, therefore, available for only a quarter of the world's nations and only for the late 1990s. Still, these data are revealing: they show a pattern of gender-based inequality in access to ICT that was still the case in the early 2000s.

Women account for varying shares of the on-line population, ranging between 51% of the local on-line population in the United States to 14% in Ethiopia. Particularly in the global core (the rich, industrialized countries such as the United States, Canada, Australia, and western Europeans nations), women's share of the on-line population is high; a close to equal share also appears in Thailand (49%), South Africa (49%), and Mexico (46%). Indeed, other than for a few poor countries (namely, Ethiopia, Senegal, and Morocco), there is not a dramatic difference in women's share of the on-line population among the countries for which data are available (Figure 3.2).

Does this mean that gender parity in the digital divide has been achieved? The facts seem counterintuitive: in spite of substantial cross-national differences in digital capacity and in spite of within-country differences between men and women, among the on-line population there is almost equal access by men and by women. I think the story here is about the availability of the data, rather than about social equality of the sexes. What we see through these data is a description of the global elite, within which women are given the same chances as men, not a tale of gender parity in the overall population in these countries and worldwide. Specifically, it is not that all women in Thailand are equal to all Thai men on all social dimensions, but rather that among the Thai elite (those who are by definition on-line and users of other advanced technologies) women's share is basically equal to that of men. It is therefore *within* the local social elite that women are catching up to men in access to digital technology. In the United States, women Internet users jumped from 38% in 1996 to 51% in 2000, and in Thailand, from 35% to 49% in the single year 1999–2000.[8] Still, this narrowing of the gender digital divide occurs only, I suspect, within the elite group. This suspicion is confirmed by information on American women, for whom data on the digital divide are

Figure 3.2

Proportion of Female Internet Users by Income, 2000 (% of total)

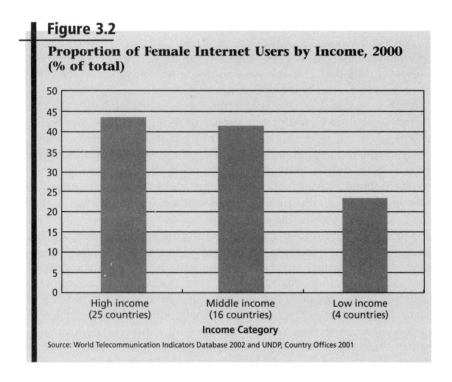

Source: World Telecommunication Indicators Database 2002 and UNDP, Country Offices 2001

relatively rich and abundant: in the United States, unmarried women and women with less than high school education are the least likely to own a computer or to have on-line access, while women with graduate degrees reached gender parity in many areas of ICT use and access.[9] I'll come back to this point in my discussion of the intersection of various digital divides.

Although these findings about the gender basis of the global digital divide are astonishing, they are not totally surprising, considering that gender is one of the "leakiest joints" in the system of education, training, and career placement. The 1999 survey of Kenyan women that showed 99% of women unaware of e-mail also showed that only one third of the women had ever been to school and less than half of these women had more than a primary education.[10] So is the social distance between women and the use of advanced technology a reflection of the relationship between women and technology in general? And is it a reflection of systemic disenfranchisement of women from sciences in general? Clearly, women who operate household gadgets such as ovens, microwaves, and toasters are using technology. The issue cannot then be that women have a natural disposition to keep their distance from technology in general. The causes must be social barriers, professional, cultural, and economic, which reflect the issue of gender-based social roles. I'll come back to the sources of social inequality later in the book, when I consider the remedies for the problem (Chapter 7).

The Racial and Ethnic Divide

Similar patterns of digital disenfranchisement are evident globally in terms of race and ethnicity. In the United States in 2000, 63% of Asian Americans and 50% of European Americans were on-line, while only 35% of African Americans and 46% of Hispanics were on-line.[11] It is not the income, education, or English-language skills that account for this difference among the racial groups in America; it is race specifically that accounts for most of the variation. As the 1999 report "Falling through the Net," published by the U.S. Department of Commerce, states: "A white, two-parent household earning less than $35,000 is nearly three times as likely to have Internet access as a comparable black household and nearly four times as likely to have Internet access as Hispanic households in the same income category."[12] Indeed, the digital race divide in the United States has been a call for action: specifically, source books such as Abdul Alkalimat's compilation of cyberspace material relevant to African Americans[13] serves as a guide to black content on the Internet, thus engaging an otherwise disenfranchised group within the digital format.

Although racial and ethnic information is not compiled in many countries, mostly because of a national ideology of a homogeneous society, there are still some reports of ethnic and racial differences in access to and use of digital technology. For example, Mexicans of European descent tend to use the Internet more frequently than indigenous people, and in Japan, ethnic Japanese tend to use digital technology more frequently than do Zainichi Koreans.

The Urban/Rural Divide

Similar to the effect of the world geographical divide on digital access, the intranational divide between urban and rural populations affects people's differential access to digital technology. Regional differentiation within countries is clear worldwide:

◆ In the Dominican Republic, 80% of all Internet users reside in the capital, Santo Domingo.[14]

◆ In Thailand, 90% of Internet users live in urban areas that are home to only 21% of the country's population.[15]

◆ In India, residents of the state of Uttar Pradesh, the province that is home to the technology hub Bangalore, have 68 times more Internet connections than residents of the state of Maharashtra, the home of the city of Mumbai, which is the financial and commercial capital of India and the most urbanized of the Indian states.[16] This gap is even more evident when Uttar Pradesh is compared with poorer and more marginal states in India.

◆ In Malaysia, only 30% of Internet subscribers live in rural areas, and in the provinces of Sabah and Semporna, where land-line telephone penetration is at 2%, Internet connections are substantially lower yet.

◆ In Bhutan, a newcomer to the Internet age, 80% of all PCs are in Thimphu, the country's capital.

Overall, then, intranational regional differences are the markings of an urban/rural divide: urban populations are more likely to have access to digital technology than are rural populations. This is true of most of the world. The exception is suburbia, which is prevalent in the United States and growing in other developed nations. In 2000 in the United States, 42% of residents of rural areas and 44% of inner-city dwellers were on-line, while 55% of residents of the suburbs were on-line. Because the American suburbs are homogeneous middle-class communities, they suck dry urban areas of affluent constituencies that are highly e-linked. As a consequence, in countries where suburbia is prevalent, the urban/rural divide is somewhat altered: rural and urban regions stand deprived, compared with suburbia.

What is the meaning of the urban/rural divide? Is residency relevant in the age of satellite communications and cybercafés at every corner? Indeed, residency is relevant to the definition of the global digital divide. In affluent countries, as in the rapidly urbanizing developing world, the residents of the inner city or city slums are further away than residents of the suburbs from digital parity. Further still from connectivity are the residents of rural areas, the romanticized, pastoral farming areas that lack exposure to modern expectations, not to mention to the necessary infrastructure. And even when cybercafés open in their vicinity, such as in Chiang Mai, Thailand, or Cusco, Peru, it is Western tourists who use these nodes into the cyberworld rather than local residents. For the locals, the cost for an hour of surfing, averaging US$2.50, may be equal to a month's wage.

"Last night we had a meal in a cybercafé just opposite the Potala. The net has come to Tibet!"

Posted by Chris Bonington, Saturday, September 5, 1998

The "Gray" Divide

On-line population worldwide is also defined in terms of age: young people are more likely than older people to utilize digital technology. Internet users who are younger than 35 account for 80% of American Internet users, 86% of Internet users in the United Kingdom, 74% of Chilean Internet users, and 84% of Chinese Internet users.[17] In Europe, where generational differences vary across countries from relatively narrow in Italy and Portugal to relatively wide in Sweden, Finland, and Denmark, the pattern is consistent across all countries: the highest share of the on-line population is people 18–25 years of age, while the lowest share is people over 65, with the age categories 26–44 and 45–64 between them.[18]

This generational gap is closely followed by industry observers: because demographic trends show that the fastest growing segment of Western societies is the "gray" group, the expectation is that in these affluent societies there may be a slowing demand for new digital technologies. Perhaps we age with the digital technology to which we were introduced and do not seek to acquire the skills for and access to newer digital media. Yet the biggest population segment in developing countries is the young: 50% of the Palestinian population, 36% of India's population, and 20% of the American population are under the age of 15. Overall, one quarter of the world's population is currently between the ages of 10 and 24, making it the largest age cohort ever to enter adulthood. This means that the IT industry may seek its future clients among the citizens of the currently marginalized countries, which are also currently poorer, less educated, less urban, and have less infrastructural base for a digital leap forward.

Education, Occupation, and Income Divides

Social differences are clearly indicated by the intertwined markers of education attainment, occupational placement, and income levels. Patterned on these markers are also differences in access to digital technology. First, higher education is a clear marker of access to and use of digital technology. In the United States, a college degree is the strongest predictor of Internet use: 74% of U.S. citizens with a college degree are on-line, whereas among those with some college education the share is 64%, among high school graduates 36%, and among those who dropped out before completing their high school education only 18%. Similar patterns emerge across the globe: 89% of Internet users in Chile, 65% in Sri Lanka, and 70% in China have college or university education.[19] Moreover, Eurobarometer

surveys from 1996 and 1999 show that the greatest rate of expansion in Internet use is among those with 20 or more years of education.[20]

Since educational attainment is closely related to occupational placement, similar patterns of digital exclusion are observed regarding workforce participation and occupational status. Across Europe, Internet use is higher among people in high-status occupations than among those in low-status occupations. Similarly, Internet use is higher among people in managerial positions than among other white-collar workers and higher still than among manual workers, home workers, and the unemployed. The gaps between these groups vary by country: the greatest gaps between high- and low-status occupations and between managerial and manual workers are in the United Kingdom and Ireland and the smallest gaps are in Greece.[21]

To some degree, occupational differences among users of digital technology vary by sector of the economy. The most pervasive use of ICT is in academia; still, whereas e-mail was first used by American academicians as early as 1972 and quickly spread among scientific institutions, scientists in developing countries still hardly rely on this technology as a mode of communication, knowledge exchange, and community buildup. Wesley Shrum, in his study of the modes of communication among scientists in three locales in developing countries—Kenya, Ghana, and the State of Karala in southwestern India—found that a mere 3% to 4% of academics had any sort of access to e-mail.[22] This means that whereas exchange and communication with peers is the core activity for scientists in keeping up with disciplinary advances and whereas knowledge exchange is considered to be a normative guideline for scientists worldwide, scientists in developing areas hardly engage in this important professional activity. The reason is primarily an absence of infrastructure to enable them to facilitate such professional exchange in a manner that has become taken for granted by scientists in developed countries. People in developing countries, scientists included, are then more isolated from their relevant worldwide community than are their Western peers or colleagues.

Income is based on occupational segmentation, and digital access is clearly differentiated by income as well. In Israel, a nation categorized as a global hub of Internet technology and dotcom activity,[23] only 19% of Israeli households in the lowest income percentile have computers, while in the highest income percentile the rate of computer ownership is 92%.[24] In Europe as a whole, wealthier households are almost three times more likely to be on-line than the poorest households: 37% of people from wealthier households were Internet users, and only 14% of members of the poorest households were on-line. In Bulgaria the poorest 65% of the population account for only 29% of Internet users.[25] Income—or alternatively poverty—is then among the strongest predictors of access to digital technology.

Summary

It is very difficult to draw a comparative picture of the global digital divide; clearly, it is difficult to segment the global digital divide by population characteristics. The problem is mainly a problem of data. Not only are there multiple dimensions of digital technology to be measured (such as Internet access, mobile phone use, PC ownership, and broadband capacity), but there are only a few sources for cross-national comparable data, based on standard definitions of such concepts as what counts as an "Internet user" or an "on-line population." Most studies draw on national reports and surveys, which are set up according to national conventions. For example, some countries count only adults among the "on-line population," whereas others include teenagers. Because Internet use is more prevalent among younger people, countries that include teenagers in their counts of Internet use report a higher ratio of on-line population than do countries that calculate the ratio in the adult population only. Similarly, some data are compiled from household surveys, while others are compiled from polling of individuals. Again, the change in the unit of analysis and the extrapolations that are made to make such data comparable have the potential to bias the findings. In spite of these clear methodological difficulties, the facts of the global digital divide are apparent. The picture emerging from the various sources points to two main patterns: (1) the digital divide comprises both access and use, and (2) the diffusion of digital technology is segmented by social characteristics.

Between Access and Use

The digital divide is composed of two forms of gaps: a gap in access to the technology and a gap in use of the technology. *Access* refers to the opportunity to reach the technology: Are there PCs available in one's vicinity? Is there an Internet connection available once a PC is accessed? If so, is the Internet connection efficient enough in terms of bandwidth to allow effective communication? *Use* refers to the rates of operation of the technology, once access is enabled. It stipulates that even when the technology is readily available for people's use, there is still apprehension about taking advantage of or relying on the technology. A recent survey of American users shows that even among regular users of computer and Internet technology, a substantive gap exists between their utilization habits. Because of limited computer skills and limited encouragement to be curious and investigative, African Americans, while sharing with European Americans positive attitudes toward high tech, tend to confine their on-line work to rudimentary tasks.[26] "The real digital divide exists between those who take advantage of the Internet to improve their lives and those who do not," concludes Ray Quay in his analysis describing the substantial differences in on-line behavior.[27] Although both dimensions describe a gap in utilization of the technology, they are substantively different. The dimension of access addresses the issues of availability and infrastructure, and the dimension of use also involves psychological readiness, individual preferences and attitudes, and personal disposition. Also, access and use empirically distinguish between opportunity and choice. Confirmed by the finding that only 20% of residents of American households with Internet connection ever went on-line,[28] it seems that indeed more people have access than use ICT.

Initial analysis of the digital divide centered exclusively on access, focusing on the availability of the technology. Only recently has the dimension (or layer) of use been added to consideration of the digital divide; use is therefore often characterized as the "second digital divide."[29] Based on these recent insights into the complexity of access to digital technology, the International Telecommunication Union (ITU) created a composite index of access, named the Digital Access Index (DAI). The efforts to compile the DAI reflect a shift in the attention paid by the international community to the problem of the global digital divide from technological achievement to access, or from a focus on advances and progress to a focus on access and equity (Box 3.1). The scale of the DAI, by portraying inequality as a continuum, responds to the critics who find the binary distinctions between the "haves" and "have-nots" too simplistic an image of social divides.[30]

Segmentation by Social Characteristics

Access to and use of digital technology are unmistakably segmented by social characteristics, both socially inherited features like age, race, and ethnicity and the acquired markers of education, occupation, and residency. The population of users is still the rich, educated, urban, and young. The profile of the average Internet user is a citizen of an OECD country, white, male, with professional skills and an advanced degree, younger than 35, from an urban center, and a speaker of English. A similar profile defines the average Chinese Internet user. In China, 70% of Internet users

Box 3.1

Digital Access Index

With the growing concern with issues of access and use of digital technologies, rather than with matters of technological achievement and prestige, international agencies turned their attention to comparative indexing of the global digital divide. Springing from such efforts was the Digital Access Index (DAI), developed by the International Telecommunication Union and showcased in 2003 as part of ITU's sponsorship of the first stage of the UN World Summit on Information Society (held in Geneva in December 2003).

DAI is indeed a better-than-ever index of access and use, even if it still fails—for lack of valid comparative data—to relate the global digital divide to social characteristics. It is calculated on the basis of eight cross-national measures, grouped into substantive dimensions or factors of this divide. (1) The number of fixed telephone subscribers per capita and (2) the number of mobile-cellular subscribers per capita indicate local infrastructure; (3) Internet access costs as percent of per capita income indicate affordability; (4) overall school enrollment and (5) adult literacy rate indicate knowledge base; (6) the number of broadband subscribers per capita and (7) the number of of international Internet bandwidths per capita indicate quality; and (8) the number of Internet users per capita indicates extent of use. Together, the index scores measure the overall ability of individuals in a country to access and use new ICT.

The index reflects a clear picture: access to and use of new ICT are more common in wealthier countries. Still, wealth is not all when it comes to ICT access and use. The oil-rich members of OPEC rank relatively lower on the DAI, so wealth and openness (political, cultural, and economic) seem to be the critical factors. Indeed, apart from Canada, all other "top ten" countries are European and Asian. Another regional distinction is, yet again, reserved for sub-Saharan Africa; these nations are markedly the least connected into the e-world. Last, the DAI gives some advantage to small countries: in spite of Malaysia's great efforts to diffuse ICT access and use, other small island nations (such as St. Kitts, Bahamas, and Malta) have quickly surpassed it in providing such access to their populations.

High access		Upper access		Middle access		Low access	
Sweden	0.85	Ireland	0.69	Belarus	0.49	Zimbabwe	0.29
Denmark	0.83	Cyprus	0.68	Lebanon	0.48	Honduras	0.29
Iceland	0.82	Estonia	0.67	Thailand	0.48	Syria	0.28
S. Korea	0.82	Spain	0.67	Romania	0.48	Papua NG	0.26
Norway	0.79	Malta	0.67	Turkey	0.48	Vanuatu	0.24
Netherlands	0.79	Czech Rep.	0.66	Macedonia	0.48	Pakistan	0.24
Hong Kong	0.79	Greece	0.66	Panama	0.47	Azerbaijan	0.24
Finland	0.79	Portugal	0.65	Venezuela	0.47	S. Tome and	
Taiwan	0.79	UAE	0.64	Belize	0.47	Principe	0.23
Canada	0.78	Macao	0.64	St. Vincent	0.46	Tajikistan	0.21
USA	0.78	Hungary	0.63	Bosnia	0.46	Equatorial	
UK	0.77	Bahamas	0.62	Suriname	0.46	Guinea	0.20
Switzerland	0.76	St. Kitts,		S. Africa	0.45	Kenya	0.19
Singapore	0.75	Nevis	0.60	Colombia	0.45	Nicaragua	0.19
Japan	0.75	Poland	0.59	Jordan	0.45	Lesotho	0.19

(continued)

High access		Upper access		Middle access		Low access	
Luxembourg	0.75	Slovak Rep.	0.59	Serbia, Montenegro	0.45	Nepal	0.19
Austria	0.75	Croatia	0.59	Saudi Arabia	0.44	Bangladesh	0.18
Germany	0.74	Bahrain	0.58	Peru	0.44	Yemen	0.18
Australia	0.74	Chile	0.58	China	0.43	Togo	0.18
Belgium	0.74	Antigua, Barbuda	0.57	Fiji	0.43	Solomon Islands	0.17
New Zealand	0.72	Barbados	0.57	Botswana	0.43	Uganda	0.17
Italy	0.72	Malaysia	0.56	Iran	0.43	Zambia	0.17
France	0.72	Lithuania	0.55	Ukraine	0.43	Myanmar	0.17
Slovenia	0.72	Qatar	0.55	Guyana	0.43	Congo	0.17
Israel	0.70	Brunei	0.54	Philippines	0.43	Cameroon	0.16
		Latvia	0.54	Oman	0.43	Cambodia	0.16
		Uruguay	0.54	Maldives	0.43	Laos	0.15
		Seychelles	0.54	Libya	0.42	Ghana	0.15
		Dominica	0.53	Dominican Rep.	0.42	Malawi	0.15
		Argentina	0.53	Tunisia	0.41	Tanzania	0.15
		Trinidad, Tobago	0.53	Ecuador	0.41	Haiti	0.15
		Bulgaria	0.53	Kazakhstan	0.41	Nigeria	0.15
		Jamaica	0.52	Egypt	0.40	Djibouti	0.15
		Costa Rica	0.52	Cape Verde	0.39	Rwanda	0.15
		St. Lucia	0.51	Albania	0.39	Madagascar	0.15
		Kuwait	0.51	Paraguay	0.39	Mauritania	0.14
		Grenada	0.50	Namibia	0.39	Senegal	0.14
		Mauritius	0.50	Guatemala	0.38	Gambia	0.13
		Russia	0.50	El Salvador	0.38	Bhutan	0.13
		Mexico	0.50	Palestine	0.38	Sudan	0.13
		Brazil	0.50	Sri Lanka	0.38	Comoros	0.13
				Bolivia	0.38	Cote d'Ivoire	0.13
				Cuba	0.38	Eritrea	0.12
				Samoa	0.37	DR Congo	0.12
				Algeria	0.37	Benin	0.12
				Turkmenistan	0.37	Mozambique	0.12
				Georgia	0.37	Angola	0.11
				Swaziland	0.37	Burundi	0.10
				Moldova	0.37	Sierra Leone	0.10
				Mongolia	0.35	Central African Republic	0.10
				Indonesia	0.34	Ethiopia	0.10
				Gabon	0.34	Guinea-Bissau	0.10
				Morocco	0.33	Chad	0.10
				India	0.32	Mali	0.09
				Kyrgyzstan	0.32	Burkina Faso	0.08
				Uzbekistan	0.31	Niger	0.04
				Vietnam	0.31		
				Armenia	0.30		

completed tertiary education, 84% are under age 35, 70% are male, and the residents of only two cities—Shanghai and Beijing—account for over 60% of all Chinese Internet users.[31] And so goes the pattern in the Netherlands.[32] This repeated and worldwide profile reflects the persistent connection between social characteristics and, in this case, access to and use of digital media.

The global digital divide is therefore an assemblage of several digital divides, a collection of intersecting digital divides. The first group of digital divides is individuals, based on group characteristics and personal abilities. In this group of digital divides are the social demarcations, now also technological demarcations, along gender, race and ethnicity, education, age, and social status lines. The second group of digital divides is among nations: countries differ in access to and use of digital technologies by their developmental state, infrastructural capabilities, and regional location. Most important, these multiple facets of the global digital divide intersect with each other to create a complex web of barriers to free and smooth global diffusion of digital technology. As discussed at length in the following text, the mounting barrier set by the cumulative and intersecting dimensions of the digital divide create a formidable obstacle to the prospects of equality and development.

The important sociological fact is that these divides—global and national, regional and local, urban and rural—clearly identify the parameters of modern technological exclusion. Digital marginality is distinctly related to parameters of education, wealth, and professional skills, as well as to health standards and political participation. Some reports identify those social features very clearly. For example, the Malaysian National Information Technology Council (NITC) lists in its *National Framework for Bridging the Digital Divide 2002* the seven most at-risk segments of the Malaysian population: rural residents (especially natives of Sabah and Sarawak), the urban poor (especially in Kuala Lumpur), women, youth, the disabled, senior citizens, and workers in small industries. In so doing, the Malaysian NITC points to the weak segments of the local population and relates these social markers to the digital divide. It confirms, then, that the contours of the digital divide follow the markings of social marginality in general. And this coupling between the markers of social hierarchy and the technological divide, which is true of Malaysia, is relevant in all other countries.

Historical changes in access to and use of digital technology clearly expand the boundaries of the digital population and thus alter the composition of this population of users. Over time, then, the demographics and the social characteristics of the users' population have diversified. Still, have the basic characteristics of the on-line population become all inclusive? The proponents of the "normalization thesis" already see signs that the composition of Web users has reached a point of reflecting the population's demographics. David Birdsell and his colleagues, in describing the changes to the social composition of Web users in the United States, remarks that "the Web reflects America much more accurately today than when the technology was in its infancy."[33,34] Others—myself included—are not convinced. In my view, the composition of the wired and digital population is still strikingly biased toward elite features: the on-line population worldwide is still unique in terms of its human resources, racial and gender composition, and social standing.

The layering of technological gaps with social divides conflates these dimensions into a single social problem, namely the problem of the digital divide. Still, what sort of social problem is it? Is the digital divide a problem of technology and of its diffusion rate or is it a social problem of social barriers and inequality?

Cyberclasses, or Transnational E-Litism

The digital divide is a case of new technologies and old inequalities, argues Pipa Norris and colleagues.[35] Technological inequalities reinforce and perpetuate existing social inequalities, based on old markers of stratification like occupation, race, wealth, and gender. And, since existing social inequalities map social classes, technological inequalities amount to *cyberclasses*. And the cumulative patterns of social stratification, which so clearly declare the digital divide, amount to parallel social cleavages. Together, they demarcate social classes: the digital "haves" and the digital "have-nots." Kenneth Keniston refers to this emerging global elite as "the digerati": these are the "beneficiaries of the enormous successful IT industry and other knowledge-based sectors of the economy such as biotechnology and pharmacology."[36]

As this long chapter makes clear, the digital divide rests on broader and greatly entrenched patterns of social stratification; these patterns of social stratification not only shape technological divides but also reflect other social demarcations and determine their trajectory. Even if the information age allows some social mobility into the new cyber-elite, many of the social features of this new class strongly reflect old and traditional social markers of inequality: "Unlike older Indian elites," writes Kenneth Keniston of Indian digerati, "the privileges of the new digerati are based not on caste, inherited wealth, family connections or access to traditional rulers, but on a combination of education, brainpower, special entrepreneurial skills, and the ability to stay on the 'cutting edge' of knowledge."[37] Social stratifying characteristics reinforce technological stratification. In this sense, it is social inequality in general that is at the heart of the digital divide.

Clearly, social capital—whether wealth, education, or literacy—accounts for technological literacy: early users of digital technology come from privileged backgrounds, marked by higher education and greater wealth. Inversely, technological exclusion, or marginality, is defined by intranational divides that reflect, perpetuate, and magnify the global digital divide. Even in the era of open networking and rapid communication technologies, social capital is still being reproduced and social closure maintained. The disadvantaged, previously marked by their distance from the economic and cultural core (as manifested by lower income, less education, and fewer social connections than those of members of the local social elite), are currently distanced from the high-tech core and its networking nodes. As mentioned earlier about e-dumping and related environmental regulations, developing nations view the adoption of international environmental restrictions (such as the Basel Convention) as "environmental imperialism" by developed states that are unfairly suppressing their economic development.

Is e-litism a form of social closure? Weber described social closure as an exclusionary practice by the social elite to reduce the chances of others to benefit from social resources or to experience mobility. The global elite is leaving behind the rest of humanity, the heterogeneous group of the global "have-nots," as a result of deepening global divides. Still, a full answer to this question depends not only on one's perspective (Weberian or Marxist, in essence) but also on the trajectory of the global digital divide: Is the digital divide growing or are we seeing a deepening of its reaches? Answers on this issue vary greatly. Clearly, even in the United States, where the number of Internet users grows by more than 30% annually, Internet access is far from reaching all walks of life equally. Only 12% of Americans were expected to be e-connected by the year 2005,[38] and currently, the disparity among American users is widening along income and resources divides.[39] The impact of intranational factors on the global Internet divide is implied in the finding that even countries that are similar in global standing and resources (such as Britain and Luxembourg or Malaysia and Vietnam) differ greatly in the rate of Internet diffusion to their populations.[40] National characteristics may explain this Internet gap among otherwise similar countries. In a cross-national comparative study, my colleague Yong Suk Jang and I showed that it is neither political nor economic

national characteristics that determine a country's connection with the e-world but rather cultural features (specifically, education and science expansion and networking with the global civil society) that determine technological embeddedness.[41]

Most important, the global digital divide is highly consequential for social development trajectories: technological marginality indicates the structure of opportunity for populations worldwide. In this sense, even the narrowing of some dimensions of the global digital divide is not sufficient to signal the coming closure of the digital divide. As shown earlier, it seems that the divide quickest to narrow is the gender gap. The persistence of the other social dimensions of the digital divide (along racial, income, and ethnic boundaries) suggests, though, that this gender parity "catch-up" is occurring only within the local elite. In other words, within the privileged group (which tends to be the wealthy, urban, and educated group), women are closing the Internet gap with men; it is doubtful, however, whether this catch-up is occurring within other social classes. And since some dimensions of the global digital divide seem to be closing slower than others, the near closing of the gap as a whole, along its various stratifying dimensions, is a distant dream.

Layers of Digital Inequality

The global digital divide is, then, a series of social divides. It is composed of intersecting cleavages of gender, race, ethnicity, education, occupation, income, age, residency, and citizenship—all layered on technological marginality. Digital inequality, then, is defined by multiple criteria of social appropriateness while also perpetuating e-litism or the breakdown into cyberclasses that are building one on another. This is what Charles Tilly calls institutionalization and sedimentation of categorical social divides, the cumulative layering of social divides.[42]

The layering of all these social markers magnifies the global digital divide into its current proportions. For example, the intersection of the national dynamics of the gender digital divide with the global dimension is particularly dramatic. It is in the poorest, least educated, and most marginalized societies that women are the smallest share of Internet users compared with men; on the list of countries with the smallest share of women on-line are Ethiopia, Senegal, and Zambia and the countries of the Arab world. Therefore, in the developing countries in which women's rights are particularly breached, women's share of the digital population is extremely low; the poorer the country is, the more distant women are from this frontier technology. In this case, global differences are layered on national gender differences to magnify and deepen the digital divide.

Similarly, in the poorest and more marginalized economies, low-status workers are the smallest part of the total population of users of digital technology. In this case of intersecting occupational status and globality, low-status or manual workers in developing countries lag behind doubly: behind their occupational peers in developed countries, as well as behind executives and white-collar workers in their own country. Clearly, white-collar workers, and especially managers, in developed countries lead in the access to digital technology: their daily, around-the-clock use of laptops, wireless Internet connections, and cellular phones is described as a work necessity, and all these digital links are offered to them wherever they travel—in airport lobbies, hotel rooms, corporate headquarters, and home and field offices. Manual workers worldwide rely more and more on digital technology in their manufacturing jobs: computers have come to dominate assembly-line production. Still, such workplace reliance on digital technology does not transfer to use of ICT for leisure or to digital literacy in general; in Europe, manual workers are on average one third as likely as managers to be on-line. At the bottom of global ICT scales are low-status or manual workers in developing countries. Their low-paying, low-skill jobs not only do not expose them to digital technology—other than in work such as Tai Chunhua's in the local e-waste site in the town of Guiyu in the province of Guangdong, China—but their pay also does not afford them access to digital ICT after hours.

The layering of social divides may have a multiplicative effect, to use a mathematical term. Simply said, layering is the further inflation of these already grave conditions of inequality: the intersection of social inequalities mushrooms into categorical divides that reflect the multifaceted dimensions of global social inequality. As a result of the layering, the stark difference between members of the global elite and members of the global periphery is compounded. Affluent and educated urbanites from rich countries are technologically light-years ahead of the rural poor in developing nations.

Overall, global marginality intersects with local marginality to deepen global disparities. The global digital divide is the sum of such intersections. Together, these layers of social divides define—if not determine—the differential access to the Internet, or technological marginality. Yet what is the allure or appeal of technological marginality that has allowed it to rise

over other dimensions of social inequality to become a call for action? How did the global Internet divide come to be perceived as a social problem requiring social attention? These are the issues discussed in the following chapter.

Notes

1. Based on a discussion by Ernest Wilson III; see http://www. Internetpolicy.org/briefing/ErnestWilson0700.html.
2. Charles Tilly (1999), *Durable Inequalities* (Berkeley: University of California Press).
3. From the publicity material of National Information Technology Awareness (NITA) events in 2000.
4. Pipa Norris, W. Lance Bennett, and Robert M. Entman (2001), *Digital Divide: Civic Engagement, Information Poverty, and the Internet Worldwide* (Cambridge, UK: Cambridge University Press).
5. See A. T. Kearney (2003, January/February), "Measuring Globalization: Who's Up, Who's Down?" *Foreign Policy,* pp. 60–72.
6. Gret Nulens, Nancy Hafkin, Leo Van Audenhove, and Bart Cammaerts (ed.) (2001), *The Digital Divide in Developing Countries: An Information Society in Africa* (Brussels: Brussels University Press).
7. To learn more about the relations of women in developing countries with technology, see Swasti Mitter and Sheila Rowbotham (eds.) (1995), *Women Encounter Technology: Changing Patterns of Employment in the Third World* (London: Routledge).
8. United Nations Development Programme (2001). *Human Development Report 2001: Making New Technologies Work for Human Development* (New York: UNDP).
9. Susan Carol Losh (2003a), "Gender and Educational Digital Chasms in Computer and Internet Access and Use over Time: 1983–2000," *IT and Society* 1(4): 73–86; Susan Carol Losh (2003b), "Gender and Educational Digital Gaps," *IT and Society* 1(5): 56–71.
10. Shanyisa Anota Khasiani (1999), "Enhancing Women's Participation in Governance: The Case of Kakamega and Makueni Districts, Kenya," in Eva-Maria Rathgeber and Edith Ofwona Adera (eds.), *Gender and the Information Revolution in Africa,* http://www.idrc/ca/books/focus/903/11-chp08.html, accessed December 28, 2004.

11. E. Fong, Barry Wellman, R. Wilkes, and M. Kew (2001), *The Double Digital Divide* (Ottawa: Office of Learning Technologies, Human Resources Development Canada).

12. National Telecommunications and Information Administration (1995), "Falling through the Net: A Survey of the 'Have-Nots' in Rural and Urban America," report (Washington, DC: NTIA).

13. Abdul Alkalimat (2004), *The African American Experience in Cyberspace: A Resource Guide to the Best Web Sites on Black Culture and History* (London: Pluto Press).

14. UNDP (2001), note 8, p. 40.

15. UNDP (2001), note 8, p. 40.

16. UNDP (2001), note 8, p. 41.

17. UNDP (2001), note 8, p. 40.

18. Norris et al., (2001), note 4, p. 84.

19. UNDP (2001), note 8, p. 40.

20. See Norris et al. (2001), note 4, p. 85.

21. See Norris et al. (2001), note 4, p. 78.

22. Wesley Shrum, forthcoming paper in *Social Studies of Science*.

23. UNDP (2001), note 8, p. 45.

24. Gwen Ackerman (2001), "Israel's Internet Don Quixote," *Jerusalem Post* (Digital Israel Section) June 5, 2001, available at http://www.jpost.com/Editions/2001/06/03/Digital/Digital.27401.html, accessed April 14, 2002.

25. UNDP (2001), p. 40.

26. Karen Mossberger, Caroline J. Tolbert, and Mary Stansbury (2003), *Virtual Inequality: Beyond the Digital Divide* (Washington, DC: Georgetown University Press).

27. Ray Quay (2001), "Bridging the Digital Divide," *Planning* 67: 12–17.

28. Amanda Lenhart, John Horrigan, Lee Rainie, Katherine Allen, Angie Boyce, Mary Madden, and Erin O'Grach (2003), *The Ever-Shifting Internet Population: A New Look at Internet Access and the Digital Divide* (Washington, DC: Pew Internet and American Life Project).

29. See Paul Attewell (2001), "The First and Second Digital Divides," *Sociology of Education* 74: 252–259; Natriello Gary (2001), "Bridging the Second Digital Divide: What Can Sociologists of Education Contribute?" *Sociology of Education* 74: 260–265.

30. Amanda Lenhart and John B. Harrigan (2003), "Re-Visualizing the Digital Divide as a Digital Spectrum," *IT and Society* 1(5):23–39.

31. UNDP (2001), note 8, p. 40.

32. Jos De Haan (2003), "IT and Social Inequality in the Netherlands," *IT and Society* 1(4): 27–45.

33. David Birdsell, Douglas Muzio, David Krane, and Amy Cottreau (1998), "Web Users Are Looking More Like America," *The Public Perspective* 9(3): 33, www.roper-center.uconn.edu/pubpr/pp93.htm.

34. See Chapter 4 for further discussion of the "normalization thesis."

35. Norris et al. (2001), note 4.

36. Kenneth Keniston (2004), "Introduction: The Four Digital Divides," in Kenneth Keniston and Deepak Kumar (eds.), *IT Experience in India: Bridging the Digital Divide* (New Delhi: Sage), p. 17.

37. Ibid.

38. UNDP (2001), note 8, p. 35.

39. Organisation for Economic Co-operation and Development (2000), *Information Technology Outlook* (Paris: OECD), p. 86.

40. See Norris et al. (1991), note 4, pp. 66, 79.

41. See Gili S. Drori and Yong Suk Jang (2003), "The Global Digital Divide: A Sociological Assessment of Trends and Causes," *Social Science Computer Review* 21(2): 144–161.

42. Tilly (1999), note 2.

4

Understanding the Conceptual Origins and Expanding the Scope

Defining the Digital Divide as a Social Problem

Technological marginality is becoming acutely clear globally; it is now well established that world regions and countries vary dramatically in their access to and use of digital technology. It is also clear that differentiated access to technology follows the contours of social status criteria: from gender and age to education and urbanity. But why is this issue of technological marginality elevated above other dimensions of social inequality to a call for action? In particular, how has the global digital divide come to be perceived as a social problem requiring social attention, and why did it, of all other technological and social divides, receive a catchy title?

Indeed, the global digital divide has received more attention than any other technological diffusion process before it. It is also clearly defined as a social problem requiring direct attention and intervention, whereas previous technological diffusion processes were not the focus of many policy discussions. The magnitude of the attention given to this newly defined social problem is clear, from UN conferences and civic engagement initiatives by for-profit IT corporations to documentation and policy texts drafted for the purpose of remedying the problem. Social inequalities have been at the center of international policy attention, but the Internet revolution, powered by rapid globalization, added a technological dimension to the discussions of growing global disparities. Moreover, discussions of the digital divide have exposed and magnified the major restructuring brought about by globalization pressures. The uneven nature of global Internet diffusion has refocused discussions on the issue of the consequences of globalization, assessing the role of social arrangements and organizations in determining the trends and the outcomes of the process of global technology diffusion. All this action raised the level of specific attention to digital technology.

The reason for the rush to conceive of this newly fashioned global social divide—the digital divide—as a social problem that requires concerted remedy is rooted in Western, now global, culture and its emphasis on certain issues as valued. Specifically, the Western, now global, values that are used as a prism for the case of the digital gaps are the ideals of progress and justice. The argument, which I advance in the following section, is that because global digital inequality "violates" norms of both progress and justice, it was rapidly identified as a "social problem." In this sense, the global digital divide emerges because it touches on the core ontological principles of modernity.

Modern thinking calls for the achievement of progress (understood to mean collective development or accumulation of resources measured mainly in economic terms) and justice (interpreted as fairness and equality in terms of access to or outcome from social resources). George Thomas and his colleagues argue that both ideals—progress and justice—are perceived as the ends or goals of human of collective social life; both are "culturally available perspectives with respect to both individual participation in society (work, voting, consuming popular culture) and the distribution of benefits of nature (income, standard of living, possession of things)."[1] And even though these ideals are Western in their philosophical and historical nature, the worldwide dominance of Western thought, powered by both imperialism and globalization, has resulted in their worldwide acceptance. Most important, these ideals serve as the interpreters of or discursive "filters" for judgment of good versus bad, normal versus deviant, social achievement versus failure.

It is in these terms, then, that the differential diffusion of digital capacity comes to be defined as a social problem: global digital inequality is a "social problem" by our value standards of development and equality. In other words, it is by these standards—the hope for development and equality—that the differential access to digital technology came to be defined as a social problem. In this sense, the identification of the global digital divide as a social problem resembles the definition of and criteria for other social problems. For example, global differences in education capacity and achievement are seen as crippling human capital development and thus economic progress, while also disenfranchising weak populations from fulfilling their potential and being empowered and thus unjust.[2] Similarly, environmental problems are defined as both inefficient management of natural resources (which threatens future use of such resources to advance development goals) and unjust exploitation of unprotected human and natural environments.[3] The common thread among these social concerns is that a global social problem is defined as one that hinders the achievement of development and justice.

How is digital technology "filtered" through these social goals of progress and justice so as to be defined as a social problem? The cultural claims in the name of progress and justice are very broad; they extend to the conditions of nations, firms, public agencies, and individuals, while also covering cultural, political, and economic spheres. Still, even within these expanded (and still expanding) claims, technology is reserved a particular, rather specific role in the achievement of related social goals.

Regarding progress, technology in general is seen as instrumental for the achievement of this social goal worldwide: technology marks human achievement and is seen as a force for upgrading future human capacity. This perception has its roots in seventeenth-century utilitarian thought. In Sir Francis Bacon's (1561–1626) novel *New Atlantis,* published in 1627, European travelers are shipwrecked on an island between the Old and the New Worlds. Their new community, told of the previous glories of the now lowly civilization on the island, uses its European knowledge of science and mastery of technology to establish an advanced community, utilizing local resources to improve orchards and harvests, to upgrade breeds of animals, and to develop medications. As a part of describing the detailed uses of mining apparatus, water and wind utilization, production lines, and mercantile activity in this prosperous new community, Bacon writes: "The end of our foundation is the knowledge of causes, and secret motions of things; and the enlarging of the bounds of human empire, to the effecting of all things possible."[4] This piece and its rich depiction of the uses of technology for establishing a prosperous community are used as symbols of the image of technology as a tool, or means, of human progress.

Digital technology, in particular, has been molded into this discursive image. Digital information and communication technology is perceived as a resource for global economic, cultural, and political integration or as a link with the world system; integration is assumed to be a principal factor in development. Integration into the wider world has two tracks: the literal track of connection between digital ICT and development and an abstract track for depicting the connection. First, digital ICT literally connects people and countries with others; digital technology accelerates trade, expedites financial transactions, and furthers prosperity that results from integration. In this sense, digital technology is a direct means of exchange of commodities and knowledge.[5] Second, digital ICT connects people and countries to others in a more abstract way by enabling the exchange of ideas and norms. In this sense, digital technology is a mode for cultural integration, broadly defined, that is assumed to bring about prosperity by encouraging openness. Through either track of integration, it is assumed that the more integrated countries and people are, the more prosperous and more modern they become. In general, the effects of the Internet on development are mediated by the role of Internet technology as a tool of integration.

The second social goal interwoven with perceptions of digital technology is social justice. Social justice is an accepted global norm based on universalistic notions that human status and related rights, privileges, and duties extend worldwide, beyond nationality, territoriality, race, gender, or other social divides. Digital technology, perceived as a cutting-edge technology on which developmental benefits depend, is defined in terms of social justice.[6] First, access to and use of digital technology are defined as yet another right and privilege that should be available to humans worldwide. As such, the diffusion of digital technology is propagated as a basic human right, and like all human rights, it should diffuse worldwide without barriers. Second, rights and ICT are intertwined through the notion of empowerment: digital ICT enables the empowerment of otherwise voiceless and powerless social groups and individuals. For example, the Internet offers cheap, easy, yet broad exposure to the claims of various social groups, as well as the ability to bypass government censorship and open information channels.[7] Last, the role of ICT as a broadcasting channel for marginal social groups and individuals serves also as a means for the delivery of other human rights, such as the right of self-determination.[8] This perception linking ICT and social justice is sometimes made more strategic and utilitarian. Because a variety of developmental benefits hinge on access to Internet technology, any barrier to the Internet is also a barrier to development. At the same time, the broader approach to the Internet as a global social problem maintains that universal access to this new social resource is required.

As a result of such assumptions, most technology policies refer to digital technology as a strategic resource or a means for development and for social justice. See, for example, how these two social goals are emphasized in the Declaration on Science and the Use of Scientific Knowledge, the concluding statement of UNESCO's World Conference on Science for the Twenty-First Century (Budapest, Hungary, 1999): "Science and technology should also be resolutely directed towards prospects for better employment, improving competitiveness and social justice. Investment in science and technology aimed both at these objectives and at a better understanding and safeguarding of the planet's natural resource base, biodiversity and life-support systems must be increased. The objective should be a move towards sustainable development strategies through the integration of economic, social, cultural and environmental dimensions."[9]

Most important, it is this longstanding, powerful, and taken-for-granted belief in ICT as a means for development and for justice that sets the stage for the mystique of digital technology in both policy circles and public opinion. And it is this mystique of digital technology that compelled the definition of any lag or gap in the unphased diffusion of digital technology as a social problem. In other words, the reign of developmentalism (or the ideal of progress) and the premium on equality and justice compel any inequality and any cause of inequality to be defined as social problems because of their direct impeding effect on both social fabric and economic development. Therefore, the global gap in access to and use of digital technology, which is clearly such a dimension of inequality and such a cause for further inequality, has been readily defined as a social problem of global proportions: the global digital divide.

In the process of defining a condition as a social problem, the case of the global digital divide is unique. The attitude toward digital technology, even if sharing the hopeful myth of utility in terms of development and input in terms of social justice, is different from the social perception of such advanced technologies as entertainment ICT or health care technologies. For example, the Internet enjoys far more credit as a source of development and social justice than do television broadcasts, which have gotten the reputation of godless entertainment. Had the Internet gotten such a reputation, there would not be such broad support for expanding access to it and furthering its uses. Still, the mystique of technology in general as determining development and social justice prospects—while divorced from the proven performance or utility of each particular technology—is the source of the Internet's global diffusion. In this sense, it is not necessarily ICT's utility but rather the images of its utility that mediate the process of defining the global digital divide as a social problem. This contradiction is exposed when comparing policy attitudes toward the global diffusion of cutting-edge digital technology with attitudes toward the global diffusion of cutting-edge medical technology. The UNDP's Human Development Report of 2001, titled *Making New Technologies Work for Human Development,* employs an even-handed approach to both the Internet and pharmaceutical advances, presenting both as critical for human development. Still, although the direct benefits from pharmaceutical advances and proliferation to global audiences are obvious and proven, new ICT is regarded with the same high esteem even if its benefits are only long-term and have shown to be elusive even in core countries. Moreover, although barriers to the global flow of medications and medical technology are a source of policy discussions (such as the negotiations among members of the Global Alliance for Vaccine and Immunization regarding the pricing of life-saving medications for developing nations), it is the global digital divide that has received an ostentatious title and that is on the agenda of international action (such as for the 2003 and 2005 World Summits on Information Society).

In summary, social perception of digital technology, which is anchored in the modern ideals of progress and justice, frames the technology as both a means and a right. As a result, any absence of free access to and use of digital technology is perceived as a global social problem, and any interruption of unphased access to and use of digital technology is defined as the cause of this global social problem, even if the barriers are a mere reflection of persistent social, nontechnological barriers. In discursive terms, as technology is filtered through our normative screens of progress and justice, the utility of the technology is assessed and defined as a means of progress and a rightful claim for justice. In this sense, technology itself is not the problem; rather, the measuring of technological achievement by social standards makes the unequal diffusion of digital technology come to be defined as the social problem of the "global digital divide." Here again the mystique of high tech propels it as a social problem further than other social resources that are also influenced by our desire for development and our concern with inequality. For example, recent "education for all" global initiatives do not enjoy the intense public attention—or the catchy title—given to the global digital divide, from front-page coverage in central newspapers to street demonstrations. It seems, then, that the global digital divide is accompanied by missionary zeal promoting the proliferation of Internet and cellular technology as modern-day salvation, namely, progress and justice.

Still, even though the importance of technological marginality has finally been elevated to international policy discussions, the breadth of the social consequences of global technological diffusion and divides (shaping the prospects of democratization, health and agriculture advances, governance of social welfare reforms, as well as industrialization and trade) stands in sharp contrast to the limited scope of the current discussions of the process, as revealed in the following section. Digital technology in such discussions has two faces: technological capacity is understood as (1) the new human capital criterion or (2) a new form of Western imperialism.

What's between Technology and Development?

The conception of the global digital divide as a social problem requiring an immediate solution arises from the widely held belief that technology is at the core of social development. Technology is taken for granted as the motor of social progress as well as the marker of human achievement. For example, we label historical eras by the human technological capacity of the time: the Stone Age is the label used to describe the long historical period when humans mastered the utilization of stone-chiseled tools (the early Paleolithic era), and the Space Age is the label for the post-1960 era when rocketry and aerotechnology allowed for human space explorations. By extension, are we now experiencing the Digital Age? And what does the change of technological era say about the possibilities and the limitations that each technology imposes on today's human development? In general, how did technology and human development come to be so tightly interconnected in our description of the human condition?

The issue here is discursive in nature. It is about the perception and conceptualization of technology as a means for development and social justice more than it is about the proven effect of technology on these social goals (discussed in Chapter 5). The belief that the Internet and development are intertwined is a taken-for-granted postulation, operating as an example of the myth of the endless utility of technological advancement. Daniel Sarewitz, in his book *Frontiers of Illusion,* traces the assumptions that fuel American public policy about science and technology. He writes:

> As a political matter, the government spends over $70 billion a year on R&D not because it cares about the abstract pursuit of knowledge but because policy makers and the public believe that progress in science and technology create societal benefits, both tangible and intangible. Military preparedness, economic growth, medical care, adequate energy resources and national prestige are among 'the most important benefits said to accrue from the new knowledge and innovation that come from the R&D system.' . . . Because the principal political justification for R&D funding is public benefit, the basis for science and technology policy can be thought of as a social contract under which the government provides support for R&D activities in return for a product—knowledge and innovation—that contributes to the common good. . . .
>
> But how is public good created from the laws of nature? . . . The laws of nature do not ordain public good (or its opposite), which can only be created when knowledge and innovation from the laboratory interact with the cultural, economic and political institutions of society. Modern science and

technology policy is therefore founded upon a leap of faith: that the transition from the controlled, idealized, context-independent world of the laboratory to the intricate, context-saturated world of society will create social benefit. . . .

An examination of the political rhetoric used to justify and explain the structure of the R&D system yields a number of powerful and oft-heard arguments that underlie and rationalize the leap of faith. . . . [T]hey have proven sufficiently resilient and compelling to ensure political acceptability of publicly funded R&D systems. These arguments are characterized here as "myths" because they are widely subscribed to and commonly repeated, even though they are not derived from well-developed empirical or theoretical foundations. They are, at root, expressions of ideology and tools of political advocacy, accepted and expressed as truth. . . . The myth of infinite benefit: more science and more technology will lead to more public good.[10]

In this work, Sarewitz reveals the myths that are at the root of our taken-for-granted belief in science. Defining *myth* in an anthropological sense (as a taken-for-granted or sacred belief rather than a falsehood), he shows that this belief is not substantiated by empirical evidence demonstrating a positive association between technological capacity and any of the goals of development. When it comes to high tech, not even UNDP and World Bank proclamations of such relationships offer more than anecdotal evidence of local high-tech booms, such as those in India and Israel.[11] Similar tales of high tech's effects on development and social justice are told of the Asian Tigers (see Box 5.1). Still, it is anecdotal tales that support the myth of the utility of technology in general and of the ground-breaking Internet technology in particular. And most important, it is these expectations that help define any digital gap as a social problem requiring action to remedy its causes and effects.

Let me highlight two specific points about this discursive coupling of technology and development. First, discussions of Internet diffusion address this technology in a purely instrumental or technical manner. Digital technology is seen as predominantly a means for enhancing modern development, not as a general cultural framework; in this sense, the Internet is not perceived as a Western cultural agenda but rather as a vehicle for Western, now global, social goals. Such a discussion leaves out of its scope any cultural influence of technological change. Sarewitz struggles with the same dilemma when discussing science and technology policy. In a move altogether utilitarian in nature, Sarewitz footnotes his discussion of such policy: "The value of science as a cultural activity—a source of intellectual liberalization, spiritual enlightenment and aesthetic satisfaction—is incalculable, but it is not a principal motivation for government's support of research and development and therefore generally beyond the scope of this book."[12] This utilitarian approach prohibits us from examining the full scope of sources and impacts that digital technology brings to modern societies. Can we truly talk of a digital age when only the developmental, mostly economic consequences have been explored or planned for? And even if there are mentions of additional social spheres that are affected by the introduction and diffusion of digital technology (like democratization and political participation), is their mention simply paying lip service to today's politically correct themes? Indeed, discussions of the social impact of the Internet amply refer to its effects on democratization and political participation, empowerment and rights, and health care delivery, in addition to economic prosperity. Still, in my opinion, this seemingly rich embedding of the social role of the Internet in a diverse list of social effects occurred because the Internet came into the discourse of developmentalism[13] only in the late 1990s, and thus it was influenced by the policy fashions of the time and the related expansion of the definition of development from purely economic terms to broader social terms. As a result—unlike policies of science, education, or earlier technologies, which were embedded in a narrowly conceived discourse of development— the digital divide is also infused with the discursive theme of rights: access to social resources, including technology, is recast as a universalistic human right (rather than solely as a barrier to progress), and any deprivation of this right is recast as an injustice (rather than solely as a failure of effective human capital upgrading).

Second, like the public approach toward scientific advances, the perception of utility is mixed with a fear of the technology's destructive consequences. This tone clearly underlies the discussions of genetically modified food, or "FrankenFood," and it also underlies the mixing of the Internet's empowering benefits with the fear of its invasive and omnipresent penetration. Motivated by such fears, governments are imposing censorship laws to protect their stability, and parents are installing Internet filters to protect their children—all under the assumption that the Internet's openness is a source of evil, transmitting political, cultural, and moral pollution. Here, the Internet's openness is both a source of empowerment (allowing all to post their voices and reach a wider community with their messages; see Chapter 6) and a source of threat to common social practices (allowing inappropriate themes to receive the same sort of broad exposure). This approach to digital technology as a double-edged sword is an expression of the "good versus bad" debate on technological progress.

In summary, current discussions of technological diffusion and the global digital divide as a social problem (1) are approached through an instrumental and utilitarian prism and (2) take a moral stand, portraying the technology as "good" or "bad." Current discussions follow a long history

of scholarly and policy discussions of technology; both utilitarianism and suspicion of change have been tainting public debates on technological change for centuries.[14] This long history is also a call for change in one's approach to technology, namely, a call to expand the scope of discussions of digital technology and of its social role and impact away from utilitarianism, away from technical matters, away from narrow policy dimensions. Since the problem of the global digital divide seems to be a mix of technical and social matters, the issue for discussion should be: What sort of social problem is the global digital divide? Is the global digital divide a problem of technology (its diffusion path, its cost, or its uses) or a social problem (of social barriers and status closure)? In other words, Which is the net through which we fall—social or technological?

Falling through Which Net?

A series of reports by the American National Telecommunications and Information Administration (NTIA) used the catchphrase "Falling through the Net" as its title.[15] Since 1995, NTIA reports popularized the notion of the digital divide and did much to explore the social markings that define it in the United States. This title also played a game of words with the different meanings of the term "net": it refers to both the technological network (Internet) and to available social services (social network). The title implies that Americans are dropping through the social services net and are not connected with the cybernet. Indeed, the close association between social characteristics and Internet use (for that matter, access to and use of digital technology in general) raises the questions: Which net are people falling through? What kind of social resources are people missing?

Information about the extent of the digital divide shows that the digital net is composed of a varied body of skills and technologies. Obviously there are the matters of access to the Internet and mastery of computer skills, but digital technology also relates to technological education, greater transparency, more intense cross-border trade that is also less reliant on natural resources, and more robust civil society structures. In other words, in addition to the social characteristics of age, gender, race, ethnicity, residency, and wealth, the social conditions of democracy, bureaucratic efficiency, and networking with global society are also associated with the extent of the digital divide. Empirical pattens clearly demonstrate this claim. Countries that are more democratic, have a more transparent and functioning bureaucracy, and have more ties with the global networks of international nongovernmental organizations also have higher rates of Internet use.

In this sense, technology per se mutually reinforces economic globalization, political participation, a higher standard of living, and so on. The convergence of these factors during the 1990s into the seemingly seamless Web obscures the lack of inherent dependence among these social spheres, or reforms. Policy makers need to "untangle" the effects and trends of the "Washington consensus" to properly identify the core factors.

What's New about the Digital Divide?

If indeed the digital divide is entangled with other social markers and if these social markers have long signaled social classes, what's new about the digital divide? How is the digital divide different from other social divides? And how is the digital divide different from technological divides before it? These questions, while addressing the recent debate over the "newness" of the features of this latest technological revolution, essentially go to the issue of proportions. They alert us to the claim that "there is nothing new under the sun" even when public concerns are mounting, social policy is initiated, and catchphrases are coined.

Recent studies, most notably Tom Standage's book *The Victorian Internet,* about the social changes that followed the introduction of telegraph technology, emphasize the similarities between previous communication revolutions and the Internet.[16] Standage treats the recent communication media as a part of the long history of human endeavor to expedite the transmission of information. The horse-riding messenger, the post service, the telegraph, the fax machine, the Internet—all such media progressively accelerated the delivery and increased the circulation of news and information. The telegraph and the Internet also share the features of making a direct and immediate impact on their social setting: cultural exchanges, family contacts, and business transactions were reformulated as a result of the introduction of these technologies. In this sense, Standage sees these technologies as revolutionary. The telegraph, much like the Internet, broke new grounds in human exchange and changed the parameters of what is perceived as possible for social interaction; the telegraph and the Internet each had similar impacts on their social environment in their time. In telling this convincing story of the similarity across communication technologies regardless of their historical context, Standage connects technology and social life throughout human history. Others, on the other hand, emphasize the rapidity of the latest technology diffusion and stress the uniqueness of such circumstances as the intensity of global trade and the reliance of social life on information. ICT and its impact on social being, they argue, are like no technology before it. So is ICT just the latest technology to experience unequal rates of diffusion in the first stages of its expansion process, which are later somewhat rectified? Is unequal distribution the "natural" first stage of every technological distribution?

Proponents of the "normalization thesis" argue that the gaps in access to ICT that we see today are merely between the "have-nows" and "have-laters." Some reach this conclusion by comparing rates of Internet diffusion with diffusion rates of previous communication technologies or of other household gadgets: Benjamin Compaine shows that while the Internet and the PC have diffused more quickly, the trend of their diffusion to date resembles that of previous technologies.[17] Based on this claim of normalization, some object to the redistributional tone of recent digital divide policies,[18] arguing that market-led initiatives and forces will eventually diffuse ICT in a way that is both "soulful and relevant."[19]

The issue of newness of technological inequalities is difficult to resolve—indeed social gaps and technological gaps narrow over time—but at the same time new divides rise to yet again mark and magnify social inequalities. It seems more a matter of proportion: Are we looking at the trends signaling closure of divides or at the new divides that emerge?

Rethinking Scope Conditions

The social problem of the global digital divide is, it seems, more than a technical difficulty of diffusion or a technical dimension of communications. Rather, it is both a deeply social condition (most of the markers of the barriers to its diffusion are social features) and a deeply socially constructed issue (it is now reframed as a global social problem).

The first social dimension of the global digital divide, namely, the social embeddedness of this condition, raises the question "What's new?" If the global digital divide merely reflects old social divides or if it merely adds another layer to old social demarcations, why does it deserve new attention? The social embeddedness of the global digital divide also begs the question of causality: Does the inequality in access to and use of new technology drive social divides, or is it a reflection of them? It seems that technology per se and social inequalities are mutually reinforcing or coconstitutive social conditions. The second social dimension of the global digital divide, the framing of this condition as a social problem, raises the question "Who drives this social construction of a global social problem?" The definition of technological inequalities as a social problem is driven by "moral entrepreneurs" and by the organizations that carry their action. Most important to this process of definition of a social problem is the filtering of this social divide by the prism of developmentalism: technological inequalities are considered problematic to the desire to achieve development.

Notes

1. George M. Thomas, John W. Meyer, Francisco O. Ramirez, and John Boli (1987), *Institutional Structure: Constituting State, Society, and the Individual* (Newbury Park, CA: Sage), p. 31.
2. See Colette Chabbott and Francisco O. Ramirez (2000), "Development and Education," in M. T. Hallinan (ed.), *Handbook of Sociology of Education* (New York: Kluwer Press), pp. 163–187.
3. See David J. Frank, Ann Hironaka, and Evan Schofer (2000), "Environmental Protection as a Global Institution," *American Sociological Review* 65: 122–127.
4. The full text of *New Atlantis* can be found at http://www.sirbacon.org/links/newatlantis.htm. The tales of harnessing technology for advancement are described in the last third of the novel.
5. See Chapter 5 for a discussion of the relationship between ICT and development.
6. This sentiment is conveyed in, for example, J. Myers (1998), "Human Rights and Development: Using Advanced Technology to Promote Human Rights in Sub-Saharan Africa," *Case Western Reserve Journal of International Law* 30(2/3): 343–371.
7. See, for example, Sajda Qureshi (1998), "Fostering Civil Associations in Africa through GOVERNET: An Administrative Reform Network," *Journal of Information Technology for Development* 8: 121–136.
8. See Chapter 6 for a discussion of the effects of ICT on empowerment, inclusion, and group identity.

9. UNESCO (1999), "Declaration on Science and the Use of Scientific Knowledge," Section 33 (World Conference on Science for the 21st Century, Budapest). Available at www.unesco.org/science/wcs/eng/declaration_e.htm.

10. Daniel Sarewitz (1996), *Frontiers of Illusion: Science, Technology, and the Politics of Progress* (Philadelphia: Temple University Press), pp. 9–10.

11. United Nations Development Programme (2001), *Human Development Report 2001: Making New Technologies Work for Human Development* (New York: UNDP); World Bank (2000), *World Development Indicators,* CD-Rom at http://www.worldbank.org/data/wdi/index.htm.

12. Sarewitz (1996), note 10, pp. 9–10.

13. For descriptions of the discursive regime of developmentalism and analyses of its constitution and effects, see Arturo Escobar (1983), *Power, Knowledge, and Discourse as Domination: The Formation of Development Discourse, 1945–1955* (Paris: UNESCO); Arturo Escobar (1995), *Encountering Development: The Making and Unmaking of the Third World* (Princeton, NJ: Princeton University Press); James Ferguson (1990), *The Anti-Politics Machine: "Development," Depoliticization, and Bureaucratic Power in Lesotho* (Cambridge: Cambridge University Press).

14. See the discussion of Luddism in Chapter 8.

15. National Telecommunications and Information Administration (1995), "Falling through the Net: A Survey of the 'Have-Nots' in Rural and Urban America" (Washington, DC: U.S. Department of Commerce, NTIA); NTIA (1998), "Falling through the Net: New Data on the Digital Divide" (Washington, DC: U.S. Department of Commerce, NTIA); NTIA (1999), "Falling through the Net: Defining the Digital Divide" (Washington, DC: U.S. Department of Commerce, NTIA); NTIA (2000), "Falling through the Net: Towards Digital Inclusion" (Washington, DC: U.S. Department of Commerce, NTIA). Available at www.ntia.doc.gov/ntiahome/digitaldivide.

16. Tom Standage (1998), *The Victorian Internet* (New York: Walker).

17. Benjamin M. Compaine (2001), "Declare the War Won," in Benjamin M. Compaine (ed.). *The Digital Divide: Facing a Crisis or Creating a Myth?* (Cambridge, MA: MIT Press), pp. 315–335.

18. M. L. Mueller (2001), "Universal Service Policies and Wealth Redistribution," in B. M. Compaine (ed.) (2001), note 14, pp. 179–187.

19. See *BusinessWeek* (2000), "How to Bridge America's Digital Divide" (editorial), May 8, 2000.

5

Hope and Despair: The Prospects of Development Based on Digitization

The Great Promise of Digital Technology

Technology, like science and education, has long been a foundation for hopes of human development. The improvements in gadgets that come from knowledge and training have long been considered the linchpin of advanced nations, from new medications that improve health and new agricultural innovations that increase crop yield to new manufacturing techniques that enhance productivity. The common notion (and common policy guideline) describes ICT as the new criterion for sophisticated manufacturing and integration into global markets. It claims that technological mastery is a requirement for any modern economy and that high tech (Internet connectivity and PC technology) is replacing older technologies (telephones and electricity) as the basis of trade and production. These expectations have been made very explicit in national plans and international declarations.

The United Nations Development Programme (UNDP), for example, has created a rather elaborate explanation of the complex relationship between technology and human development (Figure 5.1). In general, technology and human development enjoy reciprocal relations: technological change allows improved medications, communications, agricultural yields, energy supply, and manufacturing, while enhanced human knowledge and capabilities create further technological change. Technology, then, allows

Figure 5.1

Relations between Technology and Human Progress

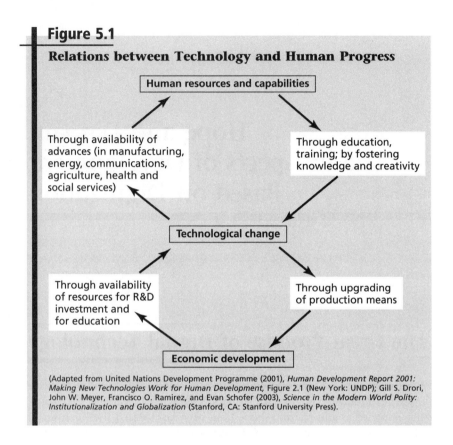

(Adapted from United Nations Development Programme (2001), *Human Development Report 2001: Making New Technologies Work for Human Development,* Figure 2.1 (New York: UNDP); Gill S. Drori, John W. Meyer, Francisco O. Ramirez, and Evan Schofer (2003), *Science in the Modern World Polity: Institutionalization and Globalization* (Stanford, CA: Stanford University Press).

people to live longer and healthier, to enjoy prosperity and a better standard of living, and to participate more easily in their community life. In this explanation, the definitions of both technology and human development are rather broad, and both technology and human capabilities contribute to economic development.

ICT fits nicely into this general explanation of technology and human development. Still, the promise of digital technology lies specifically in its ability to expand access to knowledge and information and its ability to connect people and markets, from expediting market transactions to enabling remote education and offering quick, first-hand information in times of political crises. The speech by Kofi Annan, secretary-general of the UN, before the delegates to the 2003 World Summit on Information Society (WSIS) conveys this promise:

> The liberating and democratizing power of information is as old as the Rosetta Stone or Gutenberg press. What is new today are the technologies that are dramatically accelerating its global dissemination. These technologies are a tremendous force for creating opportunities, and for integrating people and nations into the global economy. . . . For we live today in an era in which information is omnipresent, through newspapers, radio, television and the Internet; in which information is transforming the ways we live, learn, work and relate; and in which information is indispensable—for health, agriculture, education and trade, and for cultivating the engaged and learned citizenry that is essential for democracy to work.[1]

The promise of ICT is far reaching, from global integration and economic prosperity to democracy and empowerment. This promise centers on the importance of information. Through the power of ICT to disseminate information, information is seen as the core of development prospects. Through gaining access to information, gaps in development can be closed and new peaks of human progress can be reached. For example, rural villages lacking access to health care can rely on a local paramedic and a cell phone in order to receive a medical diagnosis from a doctor in a central location; remote schools can take advantage of educational programs on-line; students can access virtual libraries to enhance studies. ICT, then, is envisioned as the channel for progress. Knowledge is the basis for transforming economies, from material-intensive economies to human capital utilization, and then from human labor to human knowledge. Thus, while human capital has been the formula for development since the 1960s, currently the emphasis of development scholars has shifted toward knowledge. And whereas improvements in human capital since the 1960s have hinged on education and literacy, current emphasis on knowledge hinges on technological literacy.

Technological Literacy as the New Human Capital Criterion

Educational and scientific policies have long perceived knowledge and technological skills as human capital. Human capital approaches, which emerged in the 1960s writings of Theodore Schultz and Gary Becker, build on old notions of investment in capital (such as equipment and physical resources) to encourage future returns. Schultz and Becker introduced the new term *human capital* to draw attention to the effect of people on development and to call for investment in people's skills and the education of people as an investment in future economic growth. This new thinking was a grand breakthrough in development scholarship. At that time, the prevailing notion was the law of diminishing returns, which in its Malthusian application predicted an expansion of world poverty due to the limited nature of physical resources (such as land, water, and mining resources). Schultz's seminal address before the American Economic Association in 1960[2] and Becker's 1964 book *Human Capital*[3] changed this dire vision of world poverty: their work focused on the human component in calculations of economic growth and equated skills with resources. Because of this breakthrough, for which both Schultz and Becker were awarded the prestigious Nobel Prize in Economic Sciences (in 1979 and 1992, respectively), development policies worldwide encouraged education and skill acquisition. The 1990s brought a new force into these international and national policies; basic science, manufacturing technology, and even science and math education are still important, but equally important is the specific mastery of ICT. Countries are now ranked by the Technology Achievement Index (see Chapter 2), and global locales are graded by their ability to become hubs of the new information age economy. These new rankings encapsulate a vision of technological literacy as the new criterion for worldliness, modernity, and progress.

What does *technological literacy* actually mean? What is the bar for technological literacy? It goes beyond mere access to the technology (using or owning a personal computer) and beyond the mere skills of usage of this technology (knowing that computer orders are given through a keyboard or a mouse, knowing how to put together the parts of a PC to enable work). Rather, the notion of technological literacy extends the previous understanding of human capacity from the ability to utilize an advanced technology to the ability to understand its logic and thus the ability to problem-solve (knowing why a click on the computer's mouse does not produce the implied task). A technologically literate person, then, is familiar with the structure and function of a computer, fluent in its utilization through computer languages and software, and able to understand its intricacies so as to work out difficulties. Technological literacy is, therefore, an advanced form of human–machine interaction: it goes into the *logic* of machine use, not just into its immediate utilization. The assumption of this rather expansive definition of what constitutes technological literacy is that it is only broad and deep understanding that allows one to manipulate the machine, to extend the breadth of its uses, and therefore to innovate (rather than use) through the machine. On a conceptual level, this notion, like the understanding that engages technology in development in general, refers to an agent–individual, a proactive human.

This definition, coined by the U.S. National Research Council, sets the bar rather high. For most people, the barriers to technological literacy are still material rather than conceptual. Competency in ICT for most of humanity means such simple tasks as understanding the role of the different dials on a radio, dialing a phone, or working a PC's mouse. As a matter of policy making, achieving technological literacy is not a simple task. It "is not a matter of running wire and providing public computers; it is also a matter of ensuring that people have the requisite skills to use the technology and that they see the relevance of technology in their lives."[4]

In addition to motivational needs, literacy also means having persistence, taking advantage of continuing education, and acquiring skills as necessary to keep up with the rapid changes in ICT. A 1999 report by the National Research Council suggests that we focus on "fluency" rather than on "literacy"; "FITness," or fluency with information technology, is "a better solution to adapt to changes in the technology" and it is achieved through lifelong learning in school, in the workplace, and independently.[5]

Technological literacy, or FITness, is not a goal in itself; rather, command of technology is considered a foundation for the contributions of ICT to the ultimate social goal, namely human development. Although the goals of human progress have been explicitly encoded in the Millennium Development Goals (elaborated on in the last section of this chapter) as the eradication of hunger and poverty, achievement of social inclusion and empowerment, and ensuring of sustainability of environmental and human resources, the most explicit and immediate goal for ICT diffusion is economic growth.

ICT and Economic Growth

Building on the common notion that technological mastery is a prerequisite for economic modernization, international organizations, such as the International Monetary Fund (IMF) and World Bank, specifically warn their "clients" that any country lagging in adoption and mastery of high tech is at high risk of being marginalized economically. These recommendations are founded on the tale of the "Asian Miracle": several East Asian countries emerged as global economic players, enjoying annual growth rates of some 10% and winning the nickname Asian Tigers (Box 5.1). This economic recovery is attributed to their aggressive penetration into the cycle of technology-intensive manufacturing during the 1960s and 1970s.

The lessons from the Asian Tigers may be specific to them: recent studies suggest that the cause for their economic success may rest with state-centralized control over local markets and with the authoritarian nature of state policies and civil culture. These features are not present in the other emerging market economies that relied on ICT integration for their economic growth during the 1990s, such as India and Brazil, and they are clearly absent in the ICT hubs of Israel and Ireland. The one thing all these ICT-based economies share is a solid human capital basis set by a quality national education system.

The recent and still in-progress ICT revolution does not offer the opportunity for multiple solid studies of the impact of ICT integration on national economic development. A 2003 Harvard study found that stronger labor productivity and consequently substantial rates of economic growth result from investments in ICT, thus siding with those who focus on the virtues of the "new economy"; moreover, this study found that the positive impact of investment in ICT has paid off not only in the United States, where one of the most prosperous times in its history is attributed to the Internet boom, but also in the developed economies of Japan and Europe.[6] A 2001 report by the Organisation for Economic Co-operation and Development (OECD) shows that during the 1980s and 1990s, ICT contributed between 0.2 and 0.5 percentage points per year to economic growth, depending on the country, and that specifically during the second half of the 1990s, this contribution rose to 0.3 to 0.9 percentage points per year.[7]

This evidence is still highly specific to particular core and semiperipheral countries, to a particular era of a remarkable economic boom, to particular sectors of ICT investments, mainly in industry. Can this evidence about the effects of ICT on economic growth be generalized to other countries and specifically to poor countries and regions? And what is the impact of ICT investment on other social goals, such as the reduction of poverty and inequality? The effects of technology and surely of science on national economic development are clearly uncertain, as suggested by contradictory empirical evidence. In addition, none of the few evaluation studies shed light on the effects of ICT on personal welfare. If anything, it seems that national ICT initiatives are disconnected from the life of the individual citizens and the quality of their lives. Kenneth Keniston bluntly writes, "The boom in Bangalore is related in very complex and indirect ways, if any, to the conditions of life of the average Indian. . . . Similarly,

Box 5.1

The "Asian Miracle" from the Perspective of the Global Digital Divide

Between the years 1965 and 1990, the East Asian region grew faster than any other part of the world: the economies of the original four "Asian Tigers" (Hong Kong, Taiwan, South Korea, and Singapore) and later of the expanded list of Asian newly industrialized countries (NICs) including Malaysia, Indonesia, and Thailand grew by close to 9% annually. This seemingly miraculous economic growth is attributed to governmental policies establishing human capital foundations for sophisticated manufacturing and later launching R&D initiatives. Lee Kwan Yew, the Singaporean premier, describes in his book *From Third World to First* the emergence of Singapore as a world leader in trade and technology since the 1960s: he tells of substantial investments in science, math, and technical education, of raising public expenditure on R&D, and of national policies to liberalize trade and regulation in order to attract foreign capital. Similarly in South Korea, tertiary education enrollments rose from 15% in 1980 to 68% in 1997, with 34% of the enrollment in science and mathematics, well ahead of the average rate of 28% among OECD members.

The prosperity and national wealth in the Asian NICs translated into ICT terms. Each of these countries became a global hub of ICT activity: South Korea is a world leader in the reaches of broadband capacity, Japan has some 2,600 Internet service providers (four times the number in Australia), and Malaysia embarked on the ambitious Multimedia Super Corridor project. Japan, Singapore, South Korea, and Malaysia are in the top ten leading exporters of high-tech products; Japan, South Korea, and Singapore are ranked by the UNDP as world leaders in technology achievement.

In spite of this success in ICT terms, the prosperity did not trickle down to the region as a whole. While leading Asian countries joined the first world, they left all other Asian countries behind. The second tier of Asian countries, which includes the Philippines, Indonesia, Sri Lanka, India, and Pakistan, have a well-established Internet presence and have set national plans for expansion, but they are struggling with disseminating services in rural areas and to the urban poor. Third-tier countries, including the Internet newcomers Vietnam, Bhutan, Laos, and Cambodia, offer only a few ISPs, and Internet access is limited to big cities only. Although they receive extensive foreign aid for ICT development (for example, connecting to the Internet through Canada's International Development Research Center under a plan called Pan Asian Networking), they have a low density of telephone land-lines and cellular networks and unreliable electric supply systems.

Inequalities in ICT access and use are apparent in the countries of Asia. As mentioned in Chapter 2, the urban/rural divide is very pronounced in Asia: in China, 60% of Internet users are residents of the two cities of Shanghai and Beijing, in Thailand 90% of Internet users live in urban areas, and in Bhutan 80% of all PCs are in Thimphu, the country's capital. The "gray" divide is similarly pronounced: 80% of Chinese Internet users are between the ages of 21 and 35. Overall, then, while Asia has benefited most in economic growth and global integration from the ICT revolution, ICT is far from being equally distributed within the region, between countries and within countries.

the flourishing of Silicon Valley (and a dozen other sites of concentrated e-economic development) did little, at least in a direct way, to diminish income inequality in the U.S. or to provide medical care for those currently uncovered by insurance."[8] In light of such empirical doubts of the ICT-and-development truism, policies urging developing countries to divert their meager resources toward ICT investments should be reevaluated.

The Innovation Divide

Experts are seeking an explanation for the still ambiguous empirical support for the effect of ICT on economic development. They expect that the problem rests on "missing links," absent intermediary institutions. One such possible intermediary institution between high tech and development is innovation: a country, a corporation, and a community must be innovators of technology—rather than merely consumers of technology—to harvest the rewards. Countries, corporations, and communities vary greatly indeed by their propensity to innovate. ICT-marginalized countries and regions of the world are lacking more than ICT infrastructure, more than equal and just access to social resources. They primarily lack the ability to be initiators of technology and thus are unable to keep up with the creative leaders of the global economy and world society. For example, 48 countries, accounting for a total population of 750 million people, account for only 47 (!) of the 51,000 American patents issued to foreign inventors in 1997.[9] These countries obviously contribute a minuscule and negligible share to the world of technological innovation and are not reaping rewards from innovation. This gap among countries in the creation of new and advanced technology is recognized as the "innovation divide." The innovation divide is understood to be directly detrimental to progress. Under the "technology for progress" line of thinking (described in detail earlier in this chapter), the innovation divide determines dependency on outside sources of manufacturing technology. Once a country relies on technical advances from abroad, the royalties and fees consume a large part of the profits and doom a country to reliance on its relative advantages of low labor and manufacturing costs. Therefore, countries that use cutting-edge manufacturing technologies reap rewards in terms of high rates of high-tech exports. For example, of the top 30 high-tech exporting economies, only 11 are in the developing world. The list includes the new industrial countries of South Korea, Malaysia, Singapore, China, Mexico,

Thailand, the Philippines, Hong Kong, Brazil, Indonesia, and Costa Rica. By comparison, Arab, sub-Saharan African, and South Asian countries account for less than 5% of the world's total of high-tech export. We see, then, that technological innovation also marks integration into the world economy and thus indirectly influences national prosperity and trajectory: the top technology innovators are the affluent Western countries, the trailing innovators are the newly industrialized countries that are currently making great efforts to establish themselves as global technology hubs, and the global economic periphery is also the periphery of the world of technological innovation.

The innovation divide is the newly defined global problem. It is specified as an extension of the problem of the global digital divide, and it is identified as in need of urgent solution to limit the expansion of digital and other technological gaps. The Declaration on Science and the Use of Scientific Knowledge, the concluding statement of UNESCO's World Conference on Science for the 21st Century, specifies:

> Most of the benefits of science are unevenly distributed, as a result of structural asymmetries among countries, regions and social groups, and between the sexes. As scientific knowledge has become a crucial factor in the production of wealth, so its distribution has become more inequitable. What distinguishes the poor (be it people or countries) from the rich is not only that they have fewer assets, but also that they are largely excluded from the creation and the benefits of scientific knowledge.[10]

This innovation divide is harder to bridge than the digital divide. It is not resolved by investing in enhanced cable or satellite connections or even by providing higher quality technical education, the common solutions prescribed for the digital divide. Rather, to address the innovation divide, countries are now struggling with the notion of introducing creativity into their economic and social structures. The 2001 *Human Development Report* published by UNDP singles out creativity as the linchpin innovation and innovation as the prime solution for global technological inequality. Creativity, it argues, is a basic human trait that needs to be unleashed to further human progress: "Today's technological transformations hinge on each country's ability to unleash the creativity of its people, enabling them to understand and master technology, to innovate and to adapt technology to their own needs and opportunities."[11]

How is a national policy to unleash such inherent human creativity? Leading this self-innovative social reform is Singapore: claiming that its people routinely master the required technological skills, Singapore is now making efforts to "unleash its people's creativity" through programs of expressive art. Art, argue Singaporean officials, has the creative energy to

teach and inspire skilled workers to be creative about their work and about conceiving of new technologies. This logic is behind a policy for extensive art education in Singapore, in the hope of generating creativity and subsequently technological innovation. While this kind of solution to the innovation divide takes a bold step toward acknowledging the human component of global divides, it also stumbles on the difficulties of solving social rather than technical problems: social problems are solved through comprehensive change in the lives and minds of people, rather than by the technical fixes of plugging this and extending the line to that.

So while creativity and innovation are explored as the underlying source of the global digital divide and of the diverging impacts of countries' integration into the global e-economy, these issues are discussion items in only a few countries. The issues are relevant only to countries that have passed a certain threshold of integration into the e-economy and a certain threshold of integration of ICT. These countries—including South Korea and European countries in addition to Singapore—are all members of the exclusive club of digital nations. They are contemplating the next step following wide access to digital means. Once digitization of their nation is secured, in such ways as high connectivity rates of local companies, households, and educational institutions, they are considering how to become technology creators so as to become world leaders in technology. But for most countries, this concern is more like a far-off dream; most countries have not yet reached anywhere near international standards of connectivity (which are set at 50% within the field). For these countries, integration into global technology means relying on technology transfer as a form of international aid.

ICT and International Aid

Technology transfer has been a core feature of international aid programs for the past 50 years: donor countries and agencies have been offering technical assistance and sharing technologies with target countries and communities. Under these initiatives, donor countries have offered both technological means (from tractors to medications to whole factories) and technological knowledge (from agricultural techniques to manufacturing standards to educational skills). Donors differ in motivation, nature, and capacity, from benevolent foundations such as the Ford Foundation delivering agricultural programs and UNESCO offering its expertise in drafting national school curricula to corporations selling proprietary information on the manufacturing of medications to local factories. Although the transfer of technologies was meant to enable developing countries to leapfrog, it lacked foundations required for sustainability. Most often, technical means were transplanted without assuring their compatibility with local customs, conditions, and needs, assuming equivalency across social context where none existed. In light of these shortcomings, the philosophy of international aid was redirected toward sustainability and adaptability of transferred technology. As the old fable turned World Bank motto goes: "Give a person a fish, and you feed him for a day; teach him how to fish, and you feed him forever." Moreover, technological aid needs to be guided by comprehensive policy: "Policy—not charity—[is required] to build technological capacity in developing countries," argues UNDP.[12]

As initiatives to distribute ICT capabilities worldwide are new to the field of international aid, they have benefited from the lessons learned about technology transfer in previous decades. Current international ICT aid programs are therefore infused with the themes of sustainability and equivalency. For example, the British charity ComputerAid donated refurbished Pentium II PCs at cost (25,000 naira, or US$190), rather than as handouts, to the Nigerian nongovermental organization (NGO) Fantsuam to use in its programs targeting rural women; the fees are assumed to offer an incentive for participation and work. In addition, the allure of ICT and its promise of development are the core inducement behind international ICT aid initiatives. The promise of progress based on connectivity encourages further diffusion of ICT and greater sponsorship of ICT-aid programs. Clearly, advanced technology departs here from "old style" technologies. For example, even though there are fewer phone connections in all sub-Saharan countries combined than on the island of Manhattan and fewer cars in sub-Saharan Africa than in Manhattan, as Linda Main argues, "No one is suggesting sending more automobiles to Africa."[13]

In spite of the lessons learned, technological aid still falls short of expectations. The main shortfall has been in scope: international aid comes from numerous international organizations and agencies, each directing its attention to a particular issue and a particular target population; the result is a field of uncoordinated efforts. In addition, most efforts still fail to match technical requirements with local conditions. PC donations to Indonesian villages resulted in the computers' innards growing mold because PCs were designed to operate in climate-controlled environments; PC donations to rural Tanzania went to villages that were not connected to the nation's electrical grid system. The pressure from international donors on developing countries to modernize creates inherent gaps of logic and practice in their policies.

For example, in its Education for All (EFA) National Plan of Action of 2002, Namibia pledged that "learners will have access to, and use of, modern Information and Communication Technology by 2005," simultaneously vowing to "provide all schools with drinking water and electricity . . . and equip all schools with furniture by 2006."[14] Obviously, Namibia is setting itself unrealistic goals even if making clear efforts to modernize and to satisfy international standards for social services. The coexistence of goals in this policy for both infrastructure (electricity, water, and furniture) and cutting-edge technology (ICT access and use) and the absence of prioritization between them reveal the inherent dissonance of aid efforts in developing countries. Without dramatic changes in the strategies of international aid, there is little chance that programs for technological aid will perform any better than previous technology transfer aid programs, leaving most of humanity literally without an electrical plug, let alone the foundation in governance to adopt new technology (Box 5.2).

As has been occurring in development plans for awhile, aid strategies should move away from supply-side handouts and charity work toward sustainable progress. They should be expanded to aggressively connect marginal regions, to foster technological advancement in places other than the global core, and to rein in diasporas for the benefit of their homelands. But can countries leap over the developmental stage of industrialization to directly become information-based economies? Is it information per se that created the dotcom boom, or is it the culture of consumerism and technology that brought on this wave of economic prosperity? These questions are difficult to answer even a decade after the ICT-based economic boom.

The Pains of Progress

Evidence of the global diffusion of ICT and its effects on economic development reveals that yet again rapid progress corresponds to increased inequality. Just as the Industrial Revolution resulted in social problems of urbanization and alienation, so has the recent technological revolution of the information age brought prosperity while also drawing new lines of marginality and social disenfranchisement. People are divided today by the same technology that is aimed at uniting them; in spite of the goal of more frequent and faster connections and greater access to information, differential access to and use of ICT divide us into digital classes.

Box 5.2
International Technological Aid and Proprietary Rights

Most economists consider the protection of intellectual property rights a necessary prerequisite to the further development of international trade: the compensation for these rights provides the initiative for inventors, developers, and manufacturers to continue the laborious process of research, innovation, and development. Currently, international arrangements for the protection of intellectual property rights are anchored in TRIPS (Trade-Related Aspects of Intellectual Property), the multilateral agreement launched by the World Trade Organization (WTO) in 1995. TRIPS emerged from the consensus among WTO members that technological innovation is the paramount engine of productivity and growth; specifically, Article 7 of the TRIPS agreement specifies that "[t]he protection and enforcement of intellectual property rights should contribute to the promotion of technological innovation and to the transfer and dissemination of technology, to the mutual advantage of producers and users of technological knowledge and in a manner conducive to social and economic welfare, and to a balance of rights and obligations." Through such protections, TRIPS safeguards the short-term interests of the inventor by promulgating the need for strong patent protection, and it also protects the long-term benefits to society by allowing the imitation of the invention or new process based on the innovation after a period of 20 years (the period set for expiration of a patent). In a similar fashion and with a similar belief in the benefits, intellectual property rights are also protected by the World Intellectual Property Organization (WIPO), a United Nations agency that administers 23 international treaties on issues of intellectual property protection and advises its 179 member states on their implementation.

In spite of this careful balance between safeguarding the incentive system for innovation and allowing wide access to the proprietary technology, TRIPS has come under heavy attack. Primarily, TRIPS is cited as an exclusionary arrangement forced on all 141 WTO members by the few rich countries where innovation is concentrated to protect their profit from selling the right of use of their patented material. Accusations have been most vocal regarding medications: India and South Africa invoked TRIPS's "national emergency clause" (Article 31b) to grant compulsory licensing to domestic producers of medications in order to combat the health crisis of HIV/AIDS, thus bypassing international property rights and making the TRIPS arrangement obsolete.

These sorts of debates are also relevant to ICT. The rapid changes in the ICT field are accompanied by stiff patent protections, now enforced through TRIPS and WIPO agreements. Under these legal frameworks, ICT—from satellite to Internet and from computer hardware to software—is in the hands of its inventors for the 20-year duration of the patent. Although these protections allow recovery of investment costs by the inventors and R&D sites, they prohibit access to these technologies by developing countries and communities; the costs of procurement are prohibitive for poor communities and cash-strapped governments. So although ICT is cited as these countries' way out of poverty and economic marginality, the protection of ICT proprietary rights blocks this way to social progress. Therefore, the only access of poor countries to cutting-edge technologies is through international aid.

Figure 5.2

**Digital Access and Income Inequality, 2000
(n = 34 Countries)**

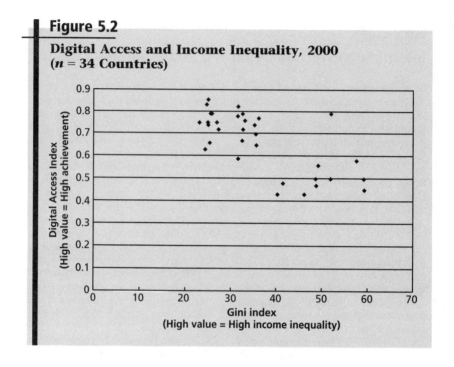

The digital divide and social inequality are intertwined. Not only is the digital divide yet another component of multifaceted social inequality, but it also corresponds empirically to standard notions of social inequality. In Figure 5.2 I plot two indicators for this relationship: differential access to ICT is indicated by ITU's Digital Access Index (see Chapter 3) and social inequality is indicated by the Gini coefficient for income distribution; both are national scores and both were developed as measures of social inequality.[15] As is evident from the figure, the digital divide and social inequality are strongly related: countries that suffer from great income disparities also suffer from deep digital divides.

Is social marginality, or greater inequality along the parameters of the revolutionary technology, a necessary "evil" of any technological progress? The "normalization thesis" postulates that over time social inequalities diminish. All new social resources are unevenly distributed when first discovered, invented, or produced, yet mass production and lower costs increasingly bring them to more people over time. What has changed between the different technological revolutions? Clearly, "methodological individualism" is more prevalent as the logic of social research and policy today than it ever has been before. It is a part of the fragmentation and rationalization of social inequalities; it is the perception of continuity of social inequalities that obscures the categorical nature of social rewards and access to social resources. It also delegitimizes any universalistic claims by pointing to the social function of inequality, and thus it also delegitimizes equity as a criterion for social goals and initiatives. Even if the normalization thesis is correct in predicting the ultimate equity of ICT diffusion, current reality mixes those expectations to engage and empower people around the world with evidence of deprivation and marginality.

Means and Ends in the Globalization of Technology

Part of the problem with the slow diffusion of ICT worldwide may rest in the inevitable process of policy making. It seems that as much as ICT is perceived as a means for achieving economic development, the achievement of e-connectivity has become an end in itself. Countries worldwide are scrambling to meet diffuse benchmarks of PCs per capita and Internet density, forgetting or ignoring the accompanying needs, whether infrastructural to e-connectivity (electrical supply and capacity or educational programs) or in delineating national priorities. The result is that some rural African schools store donated PCs because there is no electrical network to plug them into or cannot use PCs stationed in classrooms because the software is in English only. Still, in these cases, the governments can pride themselves in having supplied PCs to classrooms.

This is an example of loose coupling within the system: policy goals are divorced from practices; means are disconnected from ends. The most prevalent disconnect is between policy and practice: policies are "cheap" to draft, but programs are harder to activate and results are the hardest to achieve. With the mounting international pressure to harness ICT for development and to get rid of the global digital divide, governments are rushing to enact some actions but neglecting to follow up with the supplementary requirements. Also, as mentioned earlier, the intervention of numerous international agencies creating a disconnected field further exacerbates the problem of loose coupling.

In addition to structural problems of coordination, means are turned into goals in conditions of obscure definitions and uncertainty; such conditions are clearly present in the ICT field. Current international

recommendations set numerous paths for ICT development for countries to follow: ICT for education, ICT for business, ICT for home consumption, as well as ICT for national security, health delivery, and so on. But within each such social priority field, international recommendations are unclear about which exact technology to adopt for optimal development of the field. In education, should a country encourage PCs for individual student use? Should government establish Internet or satellite connections to encourage widespread connectivity? Should it invest in mainframe computers or PC-based networks? How should it prioritize among the primary, secondary, and tertiary education systems? All these are decisions that nag government officials worldwide.

ICT globalization is a classic case of loose coupling between policy and practice. ICT policies are springing up worldwide as a form of national enactment of international prescriptions of development, but the policies are divorced from local conditions. Because the ICT agenda is encouraged by various international agencies (some of the international players and their actions are described in Chapter 6), each enacting a particular agenda of its own, the local formation of the ICT field is partitioned along the lines of the international agendas and their programs. Since poor countries are already laboring to stay in the ICT race and to provide ICT connections to their growing populations, the problem of disconnection among ICT spheres is particularly acute in countries that rely on international technological aid. And since "beggers cannot be choosers," poor countries accept whatever international technological aid they are offered, regardless of local need or conditions. Loose coupling is primarily a result of identity enactment, of nations emulating the features of developed countries, including their policies of supplying PCs to every classroom and closing the gender digital divide. In doing so, poor and weak states are powerless to draft their own development priorities and to match their social goals with what ICT can offer in delivering the goals.

From Economic Development to Human Progress: Connecting ICT with the Millennium Goals

The discussion of ICT in relation to development sends out an urgent call for expanding the definition of development, first because the scope of the consequences, or ramifications, of the global digital divide need to be expanded to encompass a variety of dimensions of human progress, and second because for most countries ICT investments need to come after setting social priorities and after identifying ICT as the means rather than the goal of development. Developmentalism has been markedly econocentric, emphasizing economic development as the primary social goal and monitoring progress by changes in GDP and GNP. Only recently has this dominant view been challenged and the call gone out for a broadening of the scope of social goals to include democracy and rights, health and civil infrastructure, security and life preservation, environmental care, antisegregation, and equality.

The drafting of the Millennium Development Goals (MDG) was done in this spirit. Adopted by the United Nations in 2000, the MDG (1) set eight goals for human development worldwide and (2) set specific targets for each of these goals to be achieved by 2015 and to be monitored continuously until then. The progress in achieving the goals is in the hands of several international agencies, centralized by the UNDP and disseminated annually in its Human Development Report. The MDG and their target goals, as specified in the Millennium Declaration, are as follows:

Goal 1 Eradicate extreme poverty and hunger: specifically, (Target 1) to halve the number of people worldwide living on less than $1 per day and (Target 2) to halve the number of people worldwide suffering from hunger.

Goal 2 Achieve universal basic education: specifically, (Target 3) to ensure universal participation of boys and girls in a full course of primary education.

Goal 3 Promote gender equality and women's empowerment: specifically, (Target 4) to achieve gender equality in access to primary and secondary education, equalize the ratio of female/male literacy, and stop age discrimination in nonagricultural sectors.

Goal 4 Improve child health: specifically, (Target 5) to reduce infant mortality by two thirds and under-five mortality by two thirds.

Goal 5 Improve maternal health: specifically, (Target 6) to reduce maternal mortality rate by three quarters.

Goal 6 Combat HIV/AIDS, malaria, and other major diseases: specifically, (Target 7) to halt and then reverse the spread of HIV/AIDS and (Target 8) to halt and then reverse the spread of malaria and other major diseases.

Goal 7 Ensure environmental sustainability: specifically, (Target 9) to integrate the principles of sustainable development into country policies and reverse the loss of environmental resources, (Target 10) to halve the proportion of people worldwide without access to safe drinking water, and (Target 11) to achieve significant improvement in the lives of at least 100 million slum dwellers.

Goal 8 Develop a global partnership for development: specifically, (Target 12) to develop further an open, rule-based, predictable, nondiscriminatory trading and financial system, (Target 13) to address the special needs of the least developed countries, (Target 14) to address the special needs of landlocked countries and small island developing nations, (Target 15) to deal comprehensively with debt problems in developing countries, (Target 16) in cooperation with developed countries, to develop and implement strategies for youth integration into work and society, (Target 17) in cooperation with pharmaceutical companies, to provide access to affordable essential drugs in developing countries, and (Target 18) in cooperation with the private sector, to make available the benefits of new technology, especially ICT.[16]

This list of international goals and the specific dimensions and criteria to achieve the goals are still contested. Most vocal is the critique that some issues are left off this list, most obviously the international aspirations to curb population growth (specifically, to provide access for all who want them to reproductive health services) and to improve labor conditions (specifically, to enforce universal standards of a safe, secure, and empowering employment environment worldwide). Still, the specificity of the MDG and the continuous efforts to monitor progress toward their achievement are a marked improvement on previous efforts to plan for development worldwide. The MDG even improve on the UNDP's indices for human development: the human development index, the human poverty index, the gender-related development index, and the gender empowerment index, all of which combine measures of health, literacy, and standard of living.

In the concerted UN effort to achieve the MDG by 2015, ICT organizations are monitoring the contribution of ICT to meeting MDG targets, specifically addressing Target 18, which calls on ICT to service social development. Specifically, organizations such as the World Bank's InfoDev Project and ITU list the specific ways by which ICT promotes MDG. How has ICT encouraged the promotion of MDG?

Goal 1 (Target 1) Eradicate extreme poverty. Through training in ICT skills and by providing ICT means, people who now access information have been able to increase their incomes. Specifically, Grameen Bank projects of leasing cellular phones to Bangladeshi village women to rent out and supplement their income is hailed as a successful case of a microcredit project utilizing ICT. Similarly, InfoDev's B2BpriceNow.com project in the Philippines, initiated in 2002, has enabled farmers and fisherman to access market prices via a Web-based cellular phone network and to judge production and marketing strategies for the cooperative's products. (Target 2) Combat hunger. Much like its B2BpriceNow.com project in the Philippines, InfoDev's Manobi project in Senegal, initiated in January 2003, encourages increasing production yield and income with Wireless Access Protocol (WAP) and short messaging service (SMS) via cell phones, and it provides fishermen with up-to-date weather reports and market price information.

Goal 2 Achieve universal basic education. Conexiones, a Colombian NGO funded through InfoDev, links university students with primary and secondary schools to teach basic computer skills to schoolchildren, as well as to work with teachers in upgrading their teaching and computer skills. Similarly, Nepalese primary school enrollment is reported to be rising following a Web-based teacher-training program. And Studies in Information Technology Application (SITA), an Indian training project for women, is reporting that graduates of the program are teaching their newly acquired computer skills to their children.

Goal 3 Promote gender equality. Numerous ICT initiatives are aimed at providing training for women to acquire the required skills to take on new social roles. Fantsuam, a Nigerian NGO located in Kafancham (600 miles from Lagos), is using refurbished donated computers to teach women basic Internet skills and to encourage them to draw on this resource for their medical and home economics needs. Cemina, a Brazilian NGO founded in 1988, promotes women's awareness and leadership through radio broadcasts now transmitted through the Internet. For these "Cyberella" broadcasts, women are recruited to voice their opinions and report abuse conditions, and they are encouraged to launch sister programs locally. Numerous training programs (like the Bayan Loco, operating since 2001 in Nigeria, and the SITA, operating since 1996 in India) train low-income women in basic computer skills for a fee.

Goals 4, 5, and 6 Improve maternal health, improve child health, and combat HIV/AIDS, malaria, and other major diseases. The direct impact of ICT on health delivery is through both education and reporting. ITU reports that American families who regularly use the Internet rely on Web-based medical information sites for medical advice and that among these families there is a dramatic increase in infant health. InfoDev reports that improved reporting of illness and disease in Peruvian rural areas through Voxiva strengthens local health delivery by providing

advice to local health professionals in rural areas from specialists in urban centers, via its Alerta product. This material also enabled a fast response to a measles outbreak in one Peruvian province.

Goal 7 Ensure environmental sustainability. As with health, the direct impact of ICT on environmental sustainability is through the diffusion of information and the compilation of reporting. Through these means, ICT is harnessed to inform "users," or farmers, of cultivation techniques to improve yield and weather patterns to help them protect themselves and their crops from floods, and to compile information on violations of sustainability and protection plans. Specifically, for example, Pest-Net, an InfoDev project in the Pacific nation of the Solomon Islands, relies on Internet information sites and on e-messaging to inform remote communities about advanced pest control means and to post pest alerts, with the hope of increasing crop yields, enhancing food security, and increasing household income.

Goal 8 Develop global partnerships calling for the involvement of multiple stakeholders and agencies to establish a broad base for support and to ensure the success of the ICT initiatives in particular and of developmental strategies in general. The simplest way to pull together developmental resources is by drawing lessons from the record of ICT initiatives in other countries and regions. For example, the Digital Dividend Clearinghouse is a global on-line platform compiling information about social enterprises that use ICT to deliver critical tools and services to underserved communities in developing countries. It draws ideas and strategies from many partners—companies (Cisco Systems and Microsoft), development agencies (the World Bank's InfoDev), and many civil organizations—and shares these ideas with all communities.

These ICT-specific development programs tackle a variety of social sectors: education and training, social development and empowerment, business development, enabling environment (policy and regulatory frameworks), rural and agricultural development, and health care. To date, the contribution of ICT to the Millennium Goals is anecdotal, focusing on specific and small programs, most of which are too recent to truly review their impact and sustainability.[17] This is nevertheless remarkable progress from previous development projects, where specific targets and monitoring mechanisms were not established. It is clear today that development projects directly orient their initiatives toward the satisfaction of the eight goals. Most important, all such efforts clearly add a social meaning to technological development, weaving the need for technology with the promotion of social goals.

Notes

1. Kofi A. Annan (2003, December), "Welcome Message to the World Summit on Information Society," Geneva. Available at http://www.dailysummit.net/english/archives/203/12/09/kofi_annan_speaks.asp.
2. Theodore W. Schultz (1961), "Investment in Human Capital," *American Economic Review* 51(10): 1–16.
3. Gary Becker (1964), *Human Capital* (New York: Columbia University Press).
4. Organisation for Economic Co-operation and Development (2000), *Information Technology Outlook* (Paris: OECD).
5. National Research Council (1999), *Being Fluent with Information Technology* (Washington, DC: National Academy Press), p. 2.
6. See Dale Jorgenson (2003, October 25), "Information Technology and the G7 Economies," *Economist*, p. 70.
7. The report, titled "ICT Investment and Economic Growth in the 1990s: Is the US a Unique Case? A Comparative Study of 9 OECD Countries" (working paper 2001/7), was published by the Directorate for Science of the Organisation for Economic Co-operation and Development and is available at http://www.olis.oecd.org/olis/2001doc.nsf/LinkTo/DSTI-DOC(2001)7, accessed February 3, 2004.
8. Kenneth Keniston (2004), "Introduction: The Four Digital Divides," in Kenneth Keniston and Deepak Kumar (eds.), *IT Experience in India: Bridging the Digital Divide* (New Delhi: Sage), p. 29.
9. Jeffrey Sachs (2000, June 24), "A New Map of the World," *Economist*, p. 3.
10. UNESCO (1999), "Declaration on Science and the Use of Scientific Knowledge," Section 5. World Conference on Science for the 21st Century, Budapest. Available at www.unesco.org/science/wcs/eng/declaration_e.htm.
11. United Nations Development Programme (2001), *Human Development Report 2001: Making New Technologies Work for Human Development* (New York: UNDP), p. 79.
12. UNDP (2001), note 11, p. 8.
13. Linda Main (2001), "The Global Information Infrastructure: Empowerment or Imperialism?" *Third World Development* 22(1): 83–97.
14. Namibia Ministry of Education, Culture and Sport (2002), Education for All (EFA) National Plan of Action, Windhoek, Namibia. http://www.unesco.org/education/efa/db/index_national_plans.shtml, accessed February 21, 2004. I thank John M. Stoops for alerting me to this story.

15. The Gini coefficient measures income inequality on a scale of 0–1 based on the distribution of income represented in a Lorenz diagram. Developed by the Italian statistician Corrado Gini, the coefficient is calculated as the ratio of the area between the Lorenz curve (reality of inequality) and the diagonal (perfect equality).

16. United Nations (2000), "Millenium Development Goals" (New York: United Nations). Available at www.un.org/milleniumgoals/.

17. For example, Robert Kozma, Ray McGhree, Edys Quellmalz, and Dan Zalels (2004), "Closing the Digital Divide: Evaluation of the World Links Program," *International Journal of Educational Development* 24(4): 361–381.

6

Globalization Battles and ICT

"E Stands for English": The Language of E-Connectivity

In 1898, when Otto von Bismark was an old man, a journalist asked him what he took to be the decisive factor in modern history. He answered, "The fact that North Americans speak English." In retrospect, he was spot on the mark about the political and economic developments of the twentieth century, and up to now he seems to have been precise about the development of the technologies that will shape the next one.[1]

English is indeed the lingua franca of the information age; some refer to it as "globalese" to imply that it is the global common language.[2] As a global language, it has had tremendous impact on the global technologies of information and communications. While Web sites can be found in several languages, English dominates as the language of use and display of Internet content. English is the language of 84% to 87% of all Web page documents.[3] An additional 15% or so of all Web pages are in the languages of the "global core"—German, Japanese, French, Spanish, Swedish, and Italian.[4] Less than 1% of all Web pages are written and displayed in any language other than these six and English.

One obvious result of this dominance of English on the Internet is that English became a requirement for Internet "membership": indeed, 94% of Internet users are English speakers.[5] At the same time, though, only one tenth of the world's population has basic proficiency in English, leaving nine out of ten people worldwide without the ability to access the e-universe, its information, and its human contacts. English is also not the first

language of most people: Chinese, Arabic, and Hindi are the first languages, or "mother tongues" of most people, while English ranks only fourth as a first language (leading Spanish by only a few million people). English nevertheless ranks first as the second language used worldwide. Some 341,000,000 are first-language English speakers worldwide, and 508,000,000 people worldwide are speakers of English as a second language.[6] Although English is the dominant language of transnational contacts, it is not the native language for most people; English is a default option required by the nature of the digital media, not a matter of personal preferences, proficiency, or cultural heritage. Therefore, as much as it is an important social resource, English is posing a problem for non-Anglophone societies.[7] In this respect, English is a towering barrier for Internet use.

English is dominant not merely in terms of proficiency, but also in terms of logic, or reason. Digital technologies are structured around the logic of English: keyboards, search engines, and software are all organized and structured around English. The logic of the English language erases the language integrity of other languages that are not based on the Latin alphabet. How shall we use our keyboard to represent symbols other than those computerized or codified in our software? How shall we translate the sounds of one language into the standard sounds associated with the reading of the English alphabet? And how shall we computerize ideogram-based alphabets in which symbols do not represent sounds but rather objects or concepts? Although the last problem is shared among only the Japanese, Korean, and Chinese languages, the first two problems raise issues that are relevant to some 200 ethnic languages worldwide. Still, if the sheer size of the potential user populations of Japanese, Korean, and Chinese is not sufficient to overcome the use of English, what chance do the small ethnic languages have to maintain their cultural integrity in the face of the Internet? In this sense, the technological tools are transmitting cultural content; content follows form.

Therefore, even local content is filtered through English translations and English-based codification; a "foreign" language must be mastered to transmit a message. Even in multilingual societies English dominates. A recent study of language choice among the Swiss shows that the language of choice for computer-mediated *inter-Swiss* exchange is English, in spite of the national languages of German, French, Italian, and to some extent Romansh; English is, then, the pan-Swiss language.[8] Moreover, the dominance of American dotcoms and American Internet audiences is making American English the dominant English dialect, strongly perpetuating America's consumerism and cultural hegemony.

And e-translation does not solve the problem. First, translation is still a cumbersome process, slow relative to the pace of Internet diffusion and proliferation of its contents. Second, translation, even when finally available, is not accompanied by the full array of digital language-support services: for example, languages already digitized in terms of font and on-screen displays are still lacking the on-line spell-checkers, electronic thesauri, and dictionaries that aid all English writers.

Such has been the experience of the Apple Corporation initiative to create Afralpha, a digital-based language to bridge the digital gap between some 20 native West African languages and computerized technologies. Although the languages were mildly amended to be alphadigitally compatible, Afralpha lacked writing support tools and never took off as a digital bridge. In this sense, any translation still keeps within the (tight) circle of the core languages. Then, even if we smooth the translation of various ethnic and national languages in and out of English, how soon will we be able to translate between distant languages (for example, between Dzonghka, the national language of Bhutan, and Yiddish, the traditional language of European Jews) or even between related languages and dialects (for example, between Yiddish and Ladino, to bridge Ashkenazi and Sepharadi Jewish traditions)? Multilingual translation is possible when the incentive is clear; currently, such incentive is not profits but rather cultural heritage. For example, the European Union is requiring its documents, in print and on-line, to appear in all 11 languages of the union, thus encouraging smooth, quick, and proficient translation among them.

Is the circle of languages used in digital technology tightening around English? Not necessarily. The lesson drawn from the globalization of satellite broadcasts is that while English-language broadcasts overshadowed all others in the first 10 years of the technology's diffusion, today satellite broadcasts are rather diverse in terms of production sources and languages used.

A command of English is an advantage, both strategically and conceptually. Strategically, the prevalence of English even as a second language seems to be the edge that enables nations to integrate into the new e-economy. For example, former British colonies, from India and Malaysia to Hong Kong and Singapore (and Ireland), relied on the widespread command of English of their populations to became instant e-economy hubs, particularly in terms of software development and services. Few, therefore, are the e-hubs that do not have a strong linkage with the English language, and the ones that do not primarily focus on manufacturing ICT. Conceptually, the absence of immersion in English signals mental and cultural barriers to the content of the Internet.

Even image-based computer interfacing, which presumably allows non-English speakers or even illiterate people to "point and click" their way through on-screen computer images for navigation and command, is a product of the Western bias that is embedded in computer technology. We accept the icon of a garbage can to signal disposal, the icon of a stamped envelope to signal mailing, and the icon of a brown folder as a signal of directory filing. These images are relevant to modern, Western-educated people; without the same cultural context, the cultural clues, signaling a connection between a symbol and a function, are lost. These symbols are not present in the lives of people from developing countries and specifically in rural areas in these countries. In this sense, locals in non-English-speaking countries, even if they have the capacity to log onto the Internet, find the messages irrelevant and the symbols to be barriers (Box 6.1).

Box 6.1

Simputer: Bypassing Language and Cost Barriers in India

Responding to the obvious need for a low-cost computer that can be easily used by non-English speakers or illiterate people, in 1998 four IT scientists at Bangalore's Indian Institute came up with an idea for a device that would serve as an alternative to the PC in developing countries. Later developed by the not-for-profit Simputer Trust (a collaboration of the Indian Institute of Science and Encore Software Ltd and later funded through "angel" sponsors), the Simputer (for simple, inexpensive, multilingual computer) bridges several digital barriers. Priced at Rs9,000 (less than US$200), it is more affordable than even the simplest PC, and its detachable SmartCard feature (a removable component that allows personalization of contacts and filing of data) allows the Simputer to be shared by a community of users. The Simputer is also portable and works on wireless networking, so its sharing and connectivity do not require much in the way of infrastructure. Last, and most important for illiterate people, the Simputer does not rely on the traditional keyboard but rather on a set of arrow keys, touch-screen functions, and a graphical display; this way, illiteracy and no command of English cease to be barriers to digital networking and information.

The creators of Simputer envision that this handheld ICT device will be purchased by local entrepreneurs and then rented out to friends and neighbors, much as cellular phones were used as the basis for Grameen Bank programs. This way, the final barrier—price—will be overcome and locals throughout India will be able to access information and communicate messages even when they cannot afford a Simputer. Named "the poor man's PC," the Simputer was launched in 2001 in Bastar, India, where some 2,000 students shared educational software and World-Space educational broadcasts through a few Simputer devices.

The Simputer has been commercially available since 2004. To read more about and find updates on the project's progress, go to http://www.simputer.org/simputer/.

Indigenous Culture under E-Attack

The penetration of Western themes and logic through digital technology—through both its mechanics and its logic—made the attack of cultural globalization on indigenous cultures even more obvious. Daniel Mato of the Central University of Venezuela quotes the complaint of one of his interviewees, Felipe Tsenkush, the leader of the Federation of Shuar and Achuar people in Ecuador:

> Most people don't know, but it takes a lot of work to be an indigenous leader these days. One has to send and receive a lot of faxes, attend numerous international meetings; and now, one also has to learn how to handle email.[9]

As much as this sarcastic comment tells us about the embeddedness of indigenous peoples in a transnational network of activism, it also reveals the changes that information and communication technologies are bringing to remote corners of world society. But is indigenous culture truly being put on the defensive, or is it changing and being remolded to the degree that it is still indigenous in global, technology-carried terms? How authentic is the exotic "native" in this age of intense global cultural pressures?

The issue of authenticity under the mounting and homogenizing effects of globalization has received much attention from social scientists and social activists alike. The fear is that the dominance of English as the form and logic of digital technology threatens to impose linguistic and cultural uniformity on the world. Some elements of this threat are obvious and clear: the Internet, whose expansion is driven by American corporations, is a major and growing site for the growing culture of consumption. George Ritzer, in his work on the "globalization of nothing," focuses on the Internet as a prime vehicle for *grobalization*—indiscriminant and overriding growth and expansion as a part of the general move from the production of "something" (products, cultural and material, that are indigenously conceived, locally controlled, and rich in distinctive content) to the diffusion of "nothing" (centrally controlled and conceived products relatively devoid of distinctive substance).[10] The Internet, because of its Americanized nature, excels in the globalization of nothing.

In addition, the power of language over technology in the Internet age acts as a multiplier and is particularly dramatic. In both form and substance, Western logic is transmitted through technology. From the inception of digital exchange, the designation of ASCII (American Standards Code for Information Exchange) as the standard code created problems for writing in any language but English: in Latin-based languages like German and Spanish, only a few characters needed adjustment, but all non-Latin-based languages, like Greek and Chinese, suffered much greater coding problems. Clearly, the languages that are based solely on ideograms (such as the Native American and Inuit languages, where a few symbols tell whole scripts) are most in danger from an attack by digital technology. People in societies whose heritage language is not communicable through digital tools (because of font or translation issues) have to face a choice: Connect with the emerging global society or immerse themselves in their own language and culture?

This dilemma encourages the phenomenon of hybrid languages that resolve the tension between digital coding schemes and linguistic traditions and rules. Internet users adapt their native languages to English to allow an easy and efficient use of the Internet. They translate their language into English phonetically (representing the original sounds in Latin characters) or orthographically (translating some language characters into their visual equivalents in English) to maintain the flow of digital text. The hybrid languages—commonly referred to as Greeklish (the adaptation of Greek into English) or Singlish (the adaptation of Singaporean Chinese to English) and so on (Box 6.2)—represent a new *glocalization* product: a dialectic outcome of the tensions between the global and the local or the problematic amalgamation of the global and the local, as conceived by Roland Robertson.[11] Although these hybrid forms are colloquial languages, not approved by national language boards or taught in school, they are emerging as powerful means of expression, especially among youth. And the weakness of the local language market, coupled with the fact that the affluent elite who hold purchasing power are fluent in English, stops any efforts to develop software in indigenous languages.[12]

Thus, not without controversy, the control of English over the Internet (its logic and its form) is transforming local languages and thus local cultures. Computer-mediated literacy is sharpening the tension, if not the contradiction, between global networks and local identities. Technological means allow for a proliferation of "imagined communities" and turn identity, ethnicity, and community into situated affiliations. As Nimmi Hutnik explains, "With rapid modernization, technological advance, and increased mobility, it is now possible to chose one's ethnic identifications in a self-conscious way. Most people have multiple group affiliations that may be emphasized or minimized according to the situation."[13]

Are all societies subject to this danger of cultural imperialism of English and the Internet? Geoffrey Nunberg and Hinrich Schultza, both linguists with Xerox PARC, found that small countries whose populations have mastered English well are more at risk. When the number of speakers of the native language is small and locals have high competence of English, En-

Box 6.2

Greeklish, Singlish, Spanglish . . .

The necessity of having to communicate local meanings (or language) through English-based computer systems has spawned new and informal hybrid languages: Greeklish (Greek screened into English), Spanglish (Spanish + English), and Singlish (Singaporean Chinese + English). In Greeklish, for example, "c" is exchanged with "h" and "u" is exchanged with "w" to approximate the original sound.*

These languages are colloquial, or informal, languages: they are not encoded in rules and are not formalized by the local language academies. They are, however, widely used in on-line exchanges. Conceptually, these new hybrid languages combine (a) immersion in the new, tech-based global community and use of the new global technologies with (b) use of locally meaningful terminology or linguistic practices. In this sense, they highlight the communication mode of the emerging global village. These new languages express the nature of globalized identities, which are hybrid forms mediated through technologies of communication. These languages are truly *glocal* products, meshing global with local.

Technology, through the mediation of cultural content, emerges not as a neutral and passive environment; rather, it is a location for intense cultural praxis. In this case, the Internet and computer-mediated communications operate to redefine identity boundaries: they distinguish "traditional" language from Englishized language and treat the two as distinct communities. The debates about the new imputations of languages go to the heart of the globalization debate, challenging the "traditional" with the "global," the "conservative" with the "modern."

---

*Dimitris Koutsogiannis and Bessie Mitsikopoulou (2003), "Greeklish and Greekness: Trends and Discourses of 'Glocalness,'" *Journal of Computer-Mediated Communication* 9(1). Available at www.jcmc.indiana.edu.

---

glish tends to be more frequently used. Therefore, in the Netherlands and the Scandinavian nations, English-language Web pages accounted for some 30% of total Internet material accessed; in France and Germany, English-languages pages accounted for some 15% to 20%; in Latin American countries, they accounted for 10% or less.[14] This is evidence that globalization and technology go hand in hand: countries that are most globalized (or most open to the outside world through trade and exchange) are also penetrated most intensively by Internet-carried English.

But digital age language chauvinism plagues even powerful societies, and when these societies feel under E(nglish)-attack, they respond aggressively. France, a center of language chauvinism, banned the term *e-mail* from the vocabulary: in July 2003 the French Ministry of Culture announced a ban on the use of *e-mail* in all government ministries, documents, publications, or Web sites. The term, it was announced by the ministry's General Commission on Terminology and Neology, was to be replaced with the term *courrier électronique* (meaning "electronic mail"), or *courriel,* for short. The spirit of this government decision to stand against the tsunami wave of English is widely expressed. In 2000 the French president, Jacques Chirac, described the prevalence of English on the Internet as a "major risk for humanity." Still, the decision to abandon the term *e-mail* was not without controversy even in France: "Protecting the language is normal," said Marie-Christine Levet, president of the French Internet service provider Club Internet, "but e-mail's so assimilated now that no one thinks of it as American." "Courriel," she added, "would just be a new word to launch."[15] Doing so seemed to be a finger in the dam of local culture; could it hold the flooding influence of English?

What, then, can we offer to protect cultural heritage and tradition? In 1993 France, one of the strong pockets of resistance to Americanization through e-attack, put on the GATT (General Agreement on Tariffs and Trade—the predecessor of the World Trade Organization) negotiating table the provision of "cultural exceptional" conditions: it argued that with the opening of world markets, cultural products like movies and literature should be treated as protected commodities rather than as other commercial commodities. Since then, intellectual property (IP) legislation has debated the qualitative difference between cultural products and technical patents. Now that their content can be rapidly exhibited worldwide, do cultural products still have unique qualities that deserve protection?

ICT has therefore altered Western and dominant cultures as it has altered the cultures of developing societies. And just like developing countries and exotic cultures, Western societies feel inundated by the rush of ICT. ICT has taken over our imagination, penetrating the logic, inspiration, and imagery of how we conceive of our life from how we set up systems and organizations to our images of our habits and of divine powers and creation. The computer has become, therefore, a metaphor for modernity (Box 6.3).

Imperialism or Empowerment?

Technology is perceived as a tool of social goals, not as a social aim in itself. When technology is criticized, it is not technology per se but the *use* of technology that makes it a tool for evil or virtuous social goals; technology is perceived as neutral, whereas its use is socially directed. This

Box 6.3

Computer-Aided Design
Jackie Hardy

In the beginning was the number cruncher.
On the face of it darkness screened.
God had cold feet, terminal-user worry.
He searched the void, put in a warm boot.
God logged on, remembered the colon,
and there was light.

Then came the word. And the word was God
was trying to jump before He could run.
Hands on, God pressed space, split-screened heaven
and earth from the waters. At the interface
God inserted disks, backed up the system
with a graphic display.

The package had chips with everything,
so God got bold, accessed the menu in colour;
blocked the earth with green, the seas blue;
entered fish and fowl. With another byte
God updated fields, returned beasts, cattle,
and creeping things.

He opened a window, watched them browse.
God saved beasts and cattle, scanned creeping things.
Somehow there were bugs in the system.
God reprocessed data, executed, maximized;
gave creeping things another pair of legs,
a sting in the tail.

Then God created first-generation humans
in His own icon. To the female He gave
the second-generation function, the womb,
so that she might be fruitful and multiply
even unto the millionth generation.
And He called her Wombman.

Then God copied the female, cut and pasted,
deleted the womb. And the male He called Man.
God scrolled though His works, monitored progress.
God saw that it was good and that His name
was in the hi-scores. Level six ended the session.
God logged off.

From Neil Astley (ed.) (1999), *New Blood* (Newcastle upon Tyne, UK: Bloodaxe Books),
p. 199.

juxtaposition exposes the gap between imagery and perception on the one hand and real effects on the other hand. It is the real effects that drive governments to hope for prosperity from sophisticated, Internet-carried information and also to fear that world connectivity will introduce their people to harmful ideas and that they will have to censor. For example, the governments of Saudi Arabia, China, and Bhutan censor Internet connections in the name of national or religious purity. So although the power of ICT to induce cultural change in societies that adopt the presumably neutral technologies is acknowledged by all, some see it as a form of imperialism while others regard it as a tool of empowerment. This "good versus bad" debate is not a new perspective on the means of social change. It has been previously applied to science, for example. Nuclear power was perceived as either demonic (its calamitous weaponry) or meliorist (its benefits as an energy source). These days, high technology is talked about the same way.

On the digital imperialism side, high technology is seen as a pervasive form of cultural imperialism. The Internet revolution is therefore labeled "e-mperialism." The claim is that high technology—because it was invented by Western-educated technocrats and conceived of within the cultural parameters of the Western world—is a vehicle for Western ideas and ideals. From hardware to software, computer technology is diffusing Western logic. As discussed previously, the dominance of the English language in hardware and software designs imposes Latin-based logic and Western modernism on the content and form of this cultural tool. Most important, because this set of technologies is a critical factor in global integration, ICT is forcing local cultures to surrender to its mechanics and thus to its logic. In this sense, the Internet is the most powerful, most integrated form of Western domination ever, combining economic pressures with cultural oppression. From this perspective, technological gaps follow the contours of Western dominance: ICT-adopting countries are Westernizing countries. And although their "achievement" marks the surrender of their authentic and traditional social characteristics, it is also celebrated as an accomplishment by the international rankers of ICT adoption, as well as of globalization and openness. These celebrations contribute to the persistent marginalization of non-Western cultures, movements, and regimes as backward, nonmodern, and technologically challenged. In the language of Michel Foucault, knowledge, like the information technology that now mediates it, maps social power relations.[16] Much like the focus of the Frankfurt School,[17] this scholarship focuses on the study of the cultural tools for perpetuating hegemonic dominance. Through such cultural means, the emerging knowledge caste system differentiates between the adopters of technology, who are defined as successful and modern, and the laggards, who are challenged to incorporate the new technology into their traditional infrastructure and life style. This demarcation between adopters and laggards conceals the existing power relationships—based, for example, on colonial imbalances—that are the foundation of differential access to and use of technology. It also maintains the global imperialist arrangement, justifying it, for example, on trade imbalances. Through economic and political control, then, Western societies hold the power to define "modern" in terms of technological capacity.

On the e-mpowerment side, digital technology is conceived as a hopeful vehicle for information diffusion and thus for all the social benefits that rely on greater access to free and open information sources. In this postindustrial era, when knowledge is the most precious commodity, the capacity to access the frontiers of knowledge defines the new human capital; greater prospects await those who acquire access to and proficiency with computer technology and digital communications. Although some benefits are specific to development (for example, developing countries are enabled to leapfrog into the information age and integrate into the global economy without the buildup of costly infrastructure), digital technology also provides a voice with which marginalized populations can communicate their agenda and reach a widely scattered population. Through communications technology, groups can state their opinions and organize interest groups from all over the world around them. Relying on this kind of strategy to create a virtual community of activists, Saudi dissident groups discuss their vision of a new Saudi Arabia on-line, American labor unionists communicate their strategies to local unions in Latin America through e-mail, and international nongovernment environmental organizations monitor violations through e-postings by indigenous tribes around the world. The Internet, then, serves as a community builder, allowing otherwise scattered people to communicate freely.

In the process of (virtual) community-building, the dominance of English in digital information and communication does not necessarily have to come at the expense of other languages; "on the Internet, the diffusion of information is not a zero-sum game," argues Geoffrey Nunberg.[18] More frequently than ever before, Web-posted material can be quickly translated into additional languages and the translations accessed at a click of a button. Numerous Web pages of companies and interest groups that are seeking international exposure offer a language choice on their home pages. And most important, the costs of multilingual postings are negligible compared with the costs associated with multilingual printed editions. In fact, as a reflection of their multicultural identity, international organizations adhere to the custom of posting information in most, if not all, languages spoken by their members. By decree, the European Union (EU), for example, posts all on-line information in its official 11 languages, each of which is clickable also by the name of the country for which the language is the official one. The opening page of Europa (http://europa.eu.int/) has 11 repetitions of the same phrase:

La Unión Europea en línea (Spain)

Den Europæiske Union online (Denmark)

Die Europäische Union online (Germany, Austria)

Η Ευρωπαϊκή Ενωση σε απευθείας σύνδεση (Greece)

The European Union On-Line (UK, Ireland)

L'Union européenne en ligne (France, Belgium, Luxembourg)

L'Unione europea in linea (Italy)

De Europese Unie on line (Netherlands)

A União Europeia em linha (Portugal)

Euroopan unioni on-line (Finland)

Europeiska unionen på Internet (Sweden)

The EU, in declaring the 11 languages its official languages and in posting all material in all 11 of them, is making more than a symbolic gesture to its multinational character; it also preserves the day-to-day use of these languages and slows, if not stops altogether, the surrender to English/Globalese. It empowers the preservation of these languages as living languages and maintains a community of speakers. Similarly, commercial Internet purveyors cater to multilingual audiences: Yahoo! offers localized versions in French, Spanish, German, Italian, Norwegian, Swedish, Danish, Japanese, Korean, and Chinese, in addition to its widely used English language version, and Google allows its users to set their Google home page to function in any one of numerous languages, from Afrikaans, Pig Latin, and Zulu to Yiddish.

It is more than the use of language that makes these new media for communication and information into a forum for cultural exchange and community formation. These media also unite people from geographically dispersed locations around their common interest: a common heritage, a common hobby, or a common language. Israelis living in the United States can read the daily newspapers from their homeland in Hebrew, and Indians maintain family ties in e-mail between Calcutta, London, and San Jose in Hindi or Urdu. These social exchanges draw on existing social networks and are made quicker and broader in the digital age. The Internet allows "linguistic communities" to thrive: discussion groups form among speakers of a language, all sharing the warm desire to use their native or newly adopted language; as Geoffrey Nunberg reports, there are over 100 languages offered by Internet sites as forums for exchange.[19] Some exchanges can be generated through the new media: nongovernmental organizations, for example, spread their gospel through e-campaigns, thus creating a new community that is essentially a virtual interest group. Some of these campaigns offer a forum and a voice for the disenfranchised. For example, Communica hosts several alternative new media, thus offering a voice to the otherwise government-censored or the poor.[20]

The new digital media are, then, a channel of community-building, a virtual community that transcends the specifics of time and space and bridges and organizes itself around subject and interest. *Blogging*, or Web journaling, is the most explicit form of electronic community-building: a community forms around the discussion of a common issue or theme when any Internet user (once engaged, the user is referred to as a *blogger*) adds journal entries or commentary. Blogging involves a highly exclusive club of Internet users: Geoffrey Nunberg estimates that only 10% of all Internet users (themselves a small minority among humanity) are bloggers.[21] In this sense, bloggers are the elite of the global e-lite. And not surprisingly, the colloquial linguistic form of blogging is stylistically similar to the language of the urban upper-middle class: it is casual, chatty, and peppered with cultural anecdotes and name-dropping, thus implying a shared cultural capital. The Internet and other digital media offer a forum in which various communities can (re)assemble. As the following random excerpts demonstrate, the Web is a forum for communities of resistance, of solidarity, of cultural exchange, and of political consequences:

Subject: Chiapas Alert
According to Pulsar, the government is now looking for any regulation or law which could stop the Zapatistas from using Internet technology. The Zapatistas have stated that they will not allow their freedom of expression through the Internet to be taken away.
—Posted by International Freedom of Expression Exchange (IFEX) on groups.google.com (group: misc.activism.progressive) on May 1, 1998.

Help Build a Better Tomorrow for America—Support the RNC!!
You can be a part of the team working with President Bush and a Republican Congress to fully enact our compassionate conservative agenda.
If you would like to contribute by mail or fax click here. Contributions or gifts to the Republican National Committee are not deductible as charitable contributions for federal income tax purposes.
—Clicked on the Republican National Committee, Become a Member Today icon on the Web site of the GOP (http://www.gop.com/), August 15, 2003.

Subject: Hungarian Goulash
I am looking for an Hungarian style Goulash recipe.
—Posted by Missy on groups.google.com (group: rec.food.recipes) on Sunday, March 18, 2001.

Is the Internet a Tool of Governmentality?

Without doubt, ICT plays a pivotal role in cultural production and reproduction: it is changing the way cultural artifacts are recorded, transmitted, and given meaning. Is it also defacing cultural traditions and homogenizing the world in a Western mold, or is it integrating marginal regions and societies into a world of hopeful union?

Before confronting this difficult puzzle, I wish to acknowledge the most important issue in the "good versus bad" debate. This issue is that the current gap in access to and use of ICT is indeed an urgent social problem, and the issue unites the opposing perspectives on global technology diffusion. The two perspectives—the hopeful e-mpowerment and the condemning e-mperialism perspectives—are united in regarding digital inequalities as harmful to the prospects of social development. The two perspectives differ, however, on what the core problem is and thus where its remedy lies. From the e-mperialism perspective, the problem lies in the persistence of social divides, in this case global and technological in nature; colonial and economic power relations are restated in technological terms and perpetuate existing differentials. The remedy is, therefore, the end of Western domination over indigenous economies and cultures worldwide. Specific to technology, marginalized societies need to harness digital technology to their needs by adapting it to their tenets, thus breaking the link between technology and Western logic.

From the e-mpowerment perspective, gaps in access to and use of digital technology expose market imperfections in technology diffusion and result in ever-growing development gaps. The remedy lies in the liberalization of globalization to the extent that the Internet and other technologies can freely diffuse worldwide, allowing the world's margins (social and geographical) an unmediated link with world culture, trade, and political institutions. Therefore, the two perspectives, although they come from distinct theoretical and policy angles, differ only a little in their perception of the global digital divide as a social problem. Although the perspectives differ in identification of the root cause—Is it market imperfections or social power relations?—they share an understanding that the uneven diffusion of ICT is indeed a global social crisis. Because they share this issue in spite of their opposing stands in the "good versus bad" debate, we should also question the current dichotomy between e-mperialism and e-mpowerment.

This dichotomy is also problematic in its vision of a total disconnect between e-mpowerment and e-mperialsim. Whereas the current "good versus bad" debate stresses that ICT is *either* disenfranchising *or* invigorating, I see ICT as simultaneously empowering and disempowering cultural channels. Relying on Michel Foucault's notion of totalizing and individualizing, I see ICT as offering a broad audience to geographically marginal or small ethnic groups, thus giving them a global voice, while also forcing the translation of their cultural claims into the formats—conceptual and technical—that are compatible with the technology. ICT has, in my opinion, a totalizing and individualizing form of power, allowing each person a voice while also imposing on individuals a hegemonic structure.

Omnes et singulatim, translated as "all and each," is the label given to this dialectic tension; it was used by Michel Foucault as the title for a series of lectures he gave in the late 1960s on the issue of governmentality. Governmentality, which describes the hegemonic control through the machinery of the state and its logic, is the prime arena for the simultaneous totalizing and individualizing.[22] In this process, governmentality defines particularistic social entities and allows them a unique voice while also subjecting them to the homogenizing effects of scripts and technologies. Digital technologies are a perfect vehicle of modern governmentality: they allow particularistic expression while also imposing a format of logic and instruments on expression.

The Internet, for example, is a stage for particularistic claims. It offers a forum for identity assertions by individuals and groups, and its democratizing format allows anyone (who can access the technology) to profess a claim. The Internet simultaneously offers a totalizing format for such particularistic claims: the WWW Consortium requires identification in the standard form of a domain name and an IP address and it recommends a format for displaying content. Cellular phones have a similar totalizing and individualizing tone: they allow immediate and wide-reaching communications with people and sources of information while also imposing rules on the communication (for example, by requiring voice or text, rather than face-to-face, communications). In this sense, ICT serves as means in the modern dialectical process of identity formation: it allows a voice for particularistic assertions of identity (individualizing) while relying on universal rules as a format for such assertions (totalizing). Roland Robertson, in his work on "glocalization," calls this dialectic process "the universalism of particularism." In the age of globalization, where the global is regarded as a homogenizing force and the local as a unique scene, technology—like other forms of knowledge—is an instrument of power.

Notes

1. Geoffrey Nunberg (2000, March 27), "Will the Internet Always Speak English?" *American Prospect* 11(10), available at www.prospect.org.
2. David Crystal (1997), *English as a Global Language* (New York: Cambridge University Press).
3. Estimate drawn from the Babel project of the Internet Society and Pipa Norris, W. Lance Bennett, and Robert M. Entman (2001), *Digital Divide: Civic Engagement, Information Poverty, and the Internet Worldwide* (Cambridge, UK: Cambridge University Press), p. 59.
4. Internet Society (1997, June), "Web Languages Hit Parade," www.isoc.org:8080/palmares.en.html, accessed January 23, 2004.
5. Linda Main (2001), "The Global Information Infrastructure: Empowerment or Imperialism?" *Third World Development* 22(1): 94.
6. Information on language use worldwide is from the Summer Institute of Linguistics (SIL) International (http://www.sil.org/) and its Ethnologue project (http://www.ethnologue.com/).
7. Robert Phillipson (1992), *Linguistic Imperialism* (Oxford: Oxford University Press); Robert Phillipson (2003), *English-Only Europe? Challenging Language Policy* (London: Routledge).
8. Mercedes Durham (2003), "Language Choice on a Swiss Mailing List," *Journal of Computer-Mediated Communication* 9(1), available at www.jcmc.indiana.edu.
9. Daniel Mato (2000), "Transnational Networking and the Social Production of Representations of Identities by Indigenous Peoples' Organizations in Latin America," *International Sociology* 15(2): 345.
10. George Ritzer (2004), *The Globalization of Nothing* (Thousand Oaks, CA: Pine Forge), in particular, pp. 134–137.
11. Roland Robertson (1992), *Globalization: Social Theory and Global Culture* (London: Sage); Roland Robertson (1994), "Globalization and Glocalization," *Journal of International Communications* 1(1): 33–52.
12. See Harsh Kumar (2004), "Science, Technology, and the Politics of Computers in Indian Languages," in Kenneth Keniston and Deepak Kumar (eds.), *IT Experience in India: Bridging the Digital Divide* (New Delhi: Sage), pp. 140–161.
13. Hutnik is quoted in Kenton T. Wilkinson (2004), "Language Differences and Communications Policy in the Information Age," *The Information Society* 20: 220.
14. Geoffrey Nunberg (1998, October), "Languages in the Wired World,"

paper presented at "The Politics of Language and the Building of Modern Nations" conference, Institut d'Etudes Politiques de Paris.

15. Source: http://www.cnn.com/2003/TECH/ptech/07/18/france.email.ap/index.html, accessed January 23, 2004.
16. Michel Foucault (1980), *Power/Knowledge* (New York: Pantheon Books).
17. The Frankfurt School included critical thinkers who rose against the dogmatic empiricist and materialist Marxist interpretations of the early twentieth century and focused on the cultural dimensions of social production and reproduction. Among its distinguished members were Max Horkheimer, Walter Benjamin, Theodore Adorno, and Herbert Marcuse, as well as Jurgen Habermas.
18. Nunberg (2000), note 1.
19. Ibid.
20. See http://www.comunica.org/index.html, accessed January 23, 2004.
21. Nunberg (2000), note 1.
22. Michel Foucault (1991), "Governmentality," in Graham Burchell, Colin Gordon, and Peter Miller (eds.), *The Foucault Effect: Studies in Governmentality* (Chicago: University of Chicago Press), pp. 87–104.

ICT and Transnationality

The Globalization of ICT

Globalization is the dominant feature of the current era and technology is a central feature of globalization. Technological globalization means the dispersion of technology worldwide at the level of people and their daily life. It also implies technological interdependence across borders and means the structuration of technology or lack thereof as a cause of global concern and action.

Technology per se, rather than as a general social notion and mode of operation, globalizes by its devices and appliances being diffused worldwide. For example, cell phones, PCs, and satellites are increasingly used worldwide. More people in more countries rely on these gadgets for daily social interaction and for daily tasks, from cooking and learning to farming. The global diffusion of ICT is well documented. Chapter 2 describes increases in global use of ICT, and here I wish to highlight the widespread reach of ICT. ICT has heavily penetrated the business world: by 2001, 68% of all firms in the European Union relied on Internet access daily, and although in Chile only 22% of all firms had daily access, more than 60% of all Chilean medium-size firms had access.[1] Similarly, ICT has heavily penetrated the education sector. Estonia leads the world with 100% of its secondary schools having Internet access. Half the world's nations had Internet access in 50% of their secondary schools by 2002.

With the Pacific island nation of Tokelau connected to the Internet in September 2003, the number of countries linked through the Internet reached 209, essentially a universal network. Overall, ICT diffuses worldwide—or globally—at an impressive rate, bringing innovation and technical means to more people and more countries over time. Such intense technological penetration, even if still highly biased in favor of the rich and educated, allows convergence of social sectors, policies, and activities on a global scale. Technology, and particularly ICT, enables more intense interdependencies around the world. ICT allows greater immediacy of social contacts around the world, leading to greater interweaving of social life across borders and greater reliance of one place on another.

The globalization of the IT sector is a case at point. The IT sector is a prime case of global division of labor. Technology enables the worldwide allocation of production tasks while also interconnecting all these distant geographical locales into a single production line and social sphere. Currently, the IT production line consists of innovation centers (R&D centers where technology is created, such as the 46 tech hubs mentioned in Chapter 2[2]), centers of IT finance (sites of concentration of venture capital to finance innovation and production, such as Silicon Valley), manufacturing sites (locations where the components are fabricated and the gadgets are assembled, such as Costa Rica, Brazil, and Taiwan), and service sites ("outsourcing" sites, predominantly in India, which provide support to consumers like call centers, back-office processing, and technical support). Even though each site has a unique role in the production process, they all depend on each other; allocation of tasks makes each site rely on the others to fulfill the process as a whole.

While transnational American firms lower production costs by locating manufacturing sites in countries with cheaper but comparable labor and favorable trade and legal environments, they also come to depend on the situation in these countries—from legal provisions and trade regulation to labor relations—for their smooth performance and thus for their viability. At the same time, the integration of semiperipheral countries into the global IT sector makes these countries more vulnerable to fluctuations in world markets and to conditions in the finance and innovation centers. For example, Costa Rica's courting of Intel to establish a local manufacturing plant paid off in terms of employment, the national tax base, and the upgrading of local human capital, but the impact of Intel on the Costa Rican economy, amounting to over 40% of the GDP within two years of establishing the local site, made the country highly dependent on the corporate strategy and decisions of the global chip manufacturer.

Technology in general and lately ICT and the problem of the digital divide have taken on a global dimension both organizationally and discursively. Organizationally, there is a dramatic global structuration of technology: today, over 650 international organizations proclaim technology to be their main issue and target of activity, and most of them were established in the era following World War II.[3] Most interesting, all these technology-oriented international organizations, in collaborating and creating webs of world action in the technology field, target technology as a *global* matter, seeing the importance of cross-border coordination and promoting the worldwide dispersion of technology. Discursively, we regard technology as a bridge over global divides—national, cultural, and social; we therefore perceive technology as an enabler of globalization and we perceive barriers to its diffusion as a social problem. Such is the attitude toward the emerging issue of the global digital divide. As described in Chapter 3, the approach toward social divides in technology access and use is increasingly defined as a social problem of global proportions that requires attention in policy and in action. Together, these organizational webs and discursive regimes bind the world and propel the globalization of ICT. The globe has become the social horizon for technology.

The globalization of ICT has therefore been evolving on an individual and local sphere as well as on organizational and global levels, in action and in policy, in discourse and in organizational structuration, in economic as in cultural terms. In these respects, ICT is transnational, a practice, culture, and power that transcend national boundaries. ICT is therefore a clear example of globalization in three dimensions: transference (intensification of global exchange), transformation (interaction among the systemic units across different dimensions and sectors of the system to change their modes of operation when integrated), and transcendence (dissolving the divide between inside and outside on a global scale and creating an enmeshment of definitions, units, and actions—all in a co-constitutive and fluid manner).[4] So although the control of proprietary rights to ICT is mostly in the hands of international corporations and although the regulation of the global IT sector is mostly in the hands of international government organizations, it is still the hope of ICT diffusion and of closing the global digital divide that has made this issue a global matter. In this process, the dynamics of transnational organizations have a unique impact on policies.

The Role of International Organizations in Technology Globalization

One of the central features of globalization is the weaving of transnational organizational webs around issues of global concern. This has certainly been a core feature of the globalization of ICT. The worldwide diffusion of ICT is carried by a network of international organizations that target technology in general and the information society in particular as their primary concern. The current global organizational field regarding the information society, a subset of the long-established global organizational field of technology,[5] has three dominant features and one central implication; these four features are the themes of this section. First is the phenomenal rate of growth in volume of the global organizational field. Second is the variety of organizations, which have a variety of themes as their central agendas but still cooperate to create this organizational field. Third is the networking of these digital divide-minded international organizations in a single dense organizational field. And last, the most important is the impact of this intensifying global organizational field on worldwide action and policy. Later in this section I elaborate on these four features of the global organizational field regarding the information society and indirectly concerning the global digital divide.

First, with the development of advanced technological means grew the number of organizations that regard ICT as either their product or their mission. And most of the related international organizations are as recently established as digital technologies themselves. The chief international governmental organization in the field of ICT, the International Telecommunication Union (ITU), was established in 1899, one of the earliest founding dates for organizations in the general technology field, but most of the related international organizations were founded after World War II. The importance of this time in international structuration is shared with other international organizational fields and is related to the emergence of the international arena as a relevant social horizon. Still, the emergence of ICT-related organizations could not have occurred earlier: the digitization of technology is a post-World War II advance.[6] In total, some 8% of all international nongovernmental organizations name technology, broadly defined, as their core concern.[7] Today, the global organizational field related to ICT in general and to the digital divide in particular is well established and the scope of the 2003 World Summit on Information Society (WSIS) indicated the size of the field: 176 countries, 50 UN bodies and agencies, 481 nongovernmental organizations, 462 individual guests, and 97 business corporations gathered specifically to consider the topic of the global information society.

Second, the global ICT-related field is highly diverse in forms, goals, and capabilities. Again, the variety of players at the 2003 WSIS is an obvious example: they represented states and the interstate system (country representatives and UN agencies), global civil society (transnational nongovernmental organizations and private individuals), and the global business community (IT corporations and the media). This sectoral breakdown reflects the participants' divergent goals and modes of operation: for-profit and not-for-profit international organizations; hierarchical and formal and informal and grass-roots organizations; national, international, and

Box 7.1

The Work of the UN on the Global Digital Divide

The involvement of the United Nations in information started as early as 1948, with the UN Conference on the Freedom of Information in Geneva. But in spite of the important 1970s discussions on the important role of information in post-industrial society (springing from the works of Daniel Bell and Mark Porat), the UN family of organizations did not move into action until the 1990s. The International Telecommunication Union (ITU), a UN organization, raised the need for the UN to take action on the unequal spread of ICT. Following ITU's Resolution 73, taken during its 1998 meeting in Minneapolis, the matters of ICT globalization and of the global digital divide were put on the agenda of the UN Administrative Committee on Coordination (ACC, later changed to Chief Executive Board, or CEB), the advisory board of the UN. The committee decided that ITU would take the lead on the UN's behalf in arranging and coordinating the World Summit on Information Society (WSIS).

ITU's plan for a two-phase world summit was endorsed in UN General Assembly Resolution 56/183. The first phase of WSIS, held in Geneva in December 2003, brought together key stakeholders in the field to discuss important issues. At its conclusion, WSIS delegates adopted both a Declaration of Principles and a Plan for Action to guide involved parties in coordinated work to bridge the global digital divide. The second phase of WSIS, held in Tunis in November 2005, evaluated progress on the 2003 plan.

To prepare for the two WSIS conferences, three international meetings were held in Geneva (PrepCom-1 in July 2002, PrepCom-2 in July 2003, and PrepCom-3 in September 2003) and an additional meeting was held in November 2003 to resolve contentious issues. Five regional preparatory meetings were also held (in Bucharest and Bishkek, the North American and European countries; in Tokyo, the Asia-Pacific countries; in the Dominican Republic, the Latin American and Caribbean countries; and in Beirut and Cairo, the Arab countries). From these

transnational organizations; communities of individuals and conglomerates. Mostly they varied by their impact on global problems: the 2002–2003 budget of ITU equaled 341,947,736 Swiss francs (or some US$27 million), with over 61% coming from member states; the net revenue of Intel Corporation alone for that year was US$26.8 billion, and Intel's net income was US$3.1 billion. These numbers illustrate the huge difference between the funding and capacity of private and public sectors (or for-profit and not-for-profit organizations) in the technology field.

Even though international organizations in the global ICT-related field each speak for a different constituency and in the name of a unique logic, they come together to "negotiate" their shared issues. The third feature of the ICT-related global organizational field is therefore the intricate nature of the connections that create a network of ties among the international and national organizations. The tripartite network—state sector, private eight preparatory meetings emerged some 80 written documents from governments, UN bodies, and UN-accredited civil society organizations. These documents served as the basis for the drafts of the Declaration of Principles and the Plan of Action.

Two features of UN activities in general clearly influenced the work on the topic of the information society. First, the high level of bureaucratization of all UN efforts clearly shaped WSIS work. Not only was UN work initiated by one of its member organizations (ITU), which created its own bureaucratic setting and procedures, but later the UN created a formal structure to coordinate all work under ITU's leadership. For example, after ITU's work in drafting resolutions and proposals for action, a high-level summit organizing committee (HLSOC) was established, under the coordinated patronage of the UN secretary-general and the chairman of the UN Chief Executive Board for Coordination (CEB, formerly ACC). HLSOC comprised representatives of some 20 UN member organizations (such as UNDP, the World Intellectual Property Organization [WIPO], and UNESCO), as well as the directors and executives of the World Trade Organization (WTO), the World Bank, and the UN's regional secretaries. An executive secretariat, drawing staff from all related UN agencies, UN member states, private multinational corporations, and international nongovernmental organizations, was formed to reside in the ITU headquarters in Geneva. On top of all that, executive secretariats were formed for each of the host countries, Switzerland and Tunis, to coordinate the work of local authorities (from traffic police to security to hotel accommodations).

Second, to gain legitimacy for its actions, UN work increasingly involves many stakeholders, including organizations and parties from beyond the UN family of organizations and member states. This was clearly the main feature of UN work toward WSIS. WSIS gathered representatives of national governments, UN member organizations, private sector corporations, and civil society organizations. Each of these four sectors was expected to contribute sponsorship by offering staff support and funding toward the joint project. This quadripartite is now a standard composition of UN activities that aim to build a consensus on international efforts.

sector, and civil society—is the new format for global work. It is perhaps a new form of corporatism, namely, global corporatism; it brings together into policy negotiation private, public, and civil sectors, much like the previous format of policy making in welfare states.[8]

Another important feature of this global web is centralization. The interaction among the organizations are just as varied as their goals and capabilities, but the UN and its agency ITU serve as central nodes in the network. This centralization is most pronounced in interactions regarding the global digital divide, even if it directly affects production and trade to a lesser degree (Box 7.1). Overall, in spite of the tensions and variety in this network of global ICT organizations, much collaborative work is done on the global digital divide.

Last and most important is the impact of this global organizational field on states, individuals, social sectors, and the world as a whole. International organizations play a pivotal role in the socialization of different global actors into the current understanding of ICT as a global bridge. The influence of these organizations, as sources of expertise in the field as well as powerful sources of funding and sponsorship, shepherds the globalization of ICT in all its dimensions. In this capacity, international organizations serve as "teachers of norms," to use Martha Finnemore's language: they prescribe the expectations that are accepted by the international community and labor to diffuse the expectations worldwide, hence shaping both the form and the content of other international players, mostly states.[9] The path of influence of international organizations on global actors, mostly states, varies greatly, and I describe here four of the most pronounced methods of influence.

First, some international organizations exercise coercive pressure over states to encourage the penetration of ICT worldwide. For example, the International Monetary Fund (IMF) sets ICT penetration as one of the infrastructural factors allowing for economic growth: ICT enables access to information, and with information decisions are more calculated, more rational, and more effective in reaching goals; any barrier to information is a barrier to effective growth strategies. With this expectation, IMF includes ICT penetration among the conditional terms of its loans to needy countries. It recommends the liberalization of communications sectors and the initiation of computer skills workshops for professionals to upgrade local capabilities while also allowing market-driven change to diffusion rates.

Second, advocacy organizations launch "naming and shaming" campaigns to reward countries that embody the ideals of ICT-driven development and to denounce the "deviants." UNDP, for one, organizes a major publicity campaign around the publication of its annual *Human Development Report*. In its 2001 report, UNDP labored to construct the Technology Achievement Index (see Chapter 2), which publicly announced the "winners" and denounced the "losers" in technology creation. Similarly, ITU's 2003 report calculated and publicized the Technology Access Index (see Box 2.3) and rewarded countries that achieved acceptable standards of ICT penetration. In so doing, UNDP and other international organizations serve as moral entrepreneurs, highlighting global expectations (not to say norms) and encouraging members of the international community to align themselves with global expectations.

A third path for the influence of international organizations on ICT globalization is through their status as sources of capability. International ICT-oriented organizations, because they are centers of expertise on the subject, serve as sources for knowledge on reform: they readily offer blueprints showing how ICT initiatives should be executed. Again, UNDP's 2001 *Human Development Report* is a clear example. In its descriptions of trends, UNDP both defines the global dimension of the ICT gap by pointing to ICT penetration rates as an urgent social matter and anchoring this urgent matter within the framework of developmentalism. In doing so, UNDP reifies the global digital divide as a social problem and prescribes policy formulas (such as establishing diasporic networks, a legislative framework to protect proprietary rights, and school curricula to address human capital needs) to remedy the problem. Similarly, although *none* of the members of the Union of International Associations (UIA) list the global digital divide among their main goals or themes, UIA posts elaborate texts about it as a global social problem. In its detailed directories, UIA not only describes the global digital divide as a global social problem but also lists the many-layered dimensions of this urgent matter: computer illiteracy, elitist control of information technology, lack of Internet access, and informational obstacles to world trade are listed among its "world problems." In its listing of possible remedial strategies for urgent global problems, UIA increasingly lists ICT-related solutions: expanding Internet access, using the Internet for development, providing public computer centers, and connecting schools to the Internet. In so doing, even international organizations for whom ICT and the global digital divide do not relate directly to their core agenda take the social role of reifying the global social problem and prescribing solutions to it. Expert-supported (not to say expert-initiated) perception of this new social divide consolidates a global social movement of sorts and imprints social policy and action worldwide, adding the missionary tone of developmentalism to an otherwise technical agenda.

The formulation of a scripted "best practice" has important implications for the power of international organizations; let me explain them before moving on to discussing the fourth path of influence of international organizations. The first implication comes from the *process* of scripting a best-practice blueprint: What happens when the understanding of what makes a best practice changes among the experts in international organizations? Definition changes in the best-practice model and even more so the frequency of definition changes leave states bewildered about what reform to initiate. The eagerness of international experts to offer and then update their "cookie cutter" solutions results in policy confusion: countries like India encourage governmental sponsorship of the building of local technology parks while also encouraging nonprotectionist approaches to the outsourcing of IT manufacturing and services. Second, states resort to relying on best-practice documents because of conditions of uncertainty. Searching for information and guidance from international organizations is a need for most states; the absence of local know-how or resources, as well as a high level of uncertainty about the future, leads governments to rely extensively on international sources of knowledge and expertise to devise national plans. This environment of uncertain conditions, accompanied by a subscribed policy solution, leads states to also look for exemplary cases to emulate. As a result, states modify their ICT sectors in response to similar changes in the international environment, either among other states or in the intensification of international "buzz" on the issue.

The fourth path of influence of international organizations is, therefore, through the effects of "buzz" or the creation of a "density effect" by institutionalizing a critical mass of action among "partner institutions." Currently, the density of the technology-oriented field, specifically of ICT and the global digital divide, is the highest it has ever been. There is a thick and stable web of connections among various organizations (governmental or nongovernmental, development-oriented or technology-oriented, corporate or public). This dense coalition campaigns for technology diffusion, making ICT become one of the critical components of all future plans for national development and reform, while also linking this agenda to other prominent issues in world society such as human rights, security, and development.

Bringing the State Back into Technology

In spite of the growing power of nongovernmental forces and of global actors in ICT globalization, states and their governments still play a decisive role in the process of IT diffusion. In the age of globalization the state seems to be under attack from both the market and the global arenas, but the role of the state in ICT development and diffusion is unquestionable.

It is important to know that state sponsorship planted the seeds for today's digital revolution, and state sponsorship was justified by pressing national interests. Today's Internet developed out of ARPA/DARPA computational and networking projects sponsored by the U.S. government. At the time, researchers had only vague expectations of these R&D projects beyond basic research and the projects had no prospects of market viability; the prime motivation was in the field of weaponry and espionage in an era of international conflict. Today, governments face more specific prospects of rewards from this "public good" investment, as prescribed to them by the international expert organizations. With these prospects charted, many local governments sponsor initial steps toward ICT diffusion. In the Philippines, for example, the government played a central role in ICT advancement. The country's first Internet network, PHNET, was initiated in 1994 by the Department of Science and Technology and a consortium of universities. This network is now expanding to include primary and secondary schools as well as public libraries, under the new name the Philippines Science Academic and Research Network. In this work, the government takes charge of sponsorship of public goods, even if the expectation is for the market (or private sector) to carry future expansion and investment in the field.

The role of governments goes beyond offering seed sponsorship for local ICT penetration. Current science and technology policies specifically call for cooperation among government, academia, and the private sector to adjust science and technology sponsorship to the current economic wave. This policy model for tripartite cooperation in establishing technology-driven growth is commonly known as the "triple helix model,"[10] and the policy calls for governmental involvement in creating the physical sites for tripartite cooperation, in the form of technology parks.

The inspiration for the triple helix model comes from Silicon Valley: the tale of the emergence of Silicon Valley intertwines Stanford University, venture capital and industrialization, and government sponsorship of "big science" projects. Frederick Terman, Stanford University's Dean of the School of Engineering and later Provost, is credited with the consolidation of this model. He committed government funds for "big science" projects conducted at Stanford to rescue the university from a budgetary crisis but mainly to confirm his "steeples of excellence" theory by luring frontier-of-knowledge science projects and top-notch faculty. He then established Stanford as a hub for innovation and encouraged the spinning off of Stanford research projects into startup technology companies.

This narrative describes the emergence of Silicon Valley as an organic development, but government-led emulations of this model occur worldwide in the hope of replicating the success of regional knowledge-based development. Efforts by the government of India, for example, led to the 1991 establishment of India's first three technology parks in Bangalore, Pune, and Bhubaneswar. By 1999, over 21 cities in India housed technology parks, and in 2000, coordinated initiatives were centralized in the hands of the newly established Ministry of Information Technology. The Indian government enabled this development through several coordinated efforts, among them, passing laws to encourage knowledge-based economic change, sponsoring upgrades to India's telecommunications infrastructure, offering tax benefits to foreign corporations seeking to expand their global operations into India, and subsidizing an excellent education system to

134

maintain the lure of India's highly skilled and English-speaking workforce. Some initiatives took a legal form, in anticipation of "trickle-down" effects. For example, the 1984 New Computer Act and the 1996 Policy on Computer Software Export, Software Development, and Training—both aimed at developing the local software sector by, for example, relaxing the tax regime for imported computer hardware—are credited with the advancement of local industry.

Although in some countries governments have initiated technology projects in industry, education, and public administration, other governments have served as barriers to intensive ICT diffusion. Through government censorship, national authorities control the flow of information and restrict access to the full scope of ICTs depending on government interests. Government control over information is seen in all countries, varying by degrees of openness of society and regime. In Singapore, which is one of the most "wired" countries in the world and a leader in high-tech exports, there are only three ISPs, and the Singaporean government owns both of the country's two broadcasting companies, dominates the telecom market through Singapore Telecom, the only telecommunications in Singapore, and controls print media through ownership of the single print outlet, Singapore Press Holdings. (In comparison, in the Philippines there are 145 ISPs, 17 newspaper organizations, and more than 100 local television stations, and the local telecom market has been privatized and opened to foreign penetration). Similarly, the government of Bhutan, which has always limited incoming tourism, controls all telecom operations. The Division of Telecommunications in Bhutan's Ministry of Communications funds, operates, and maintains all digital ICT networks. Even though ICTs are transnational in scope and dynamics and have the power to transcend national boundaries, the reaches of these technologies is still under clear control of national interests in some countries. National control is mostly in the hands of local governments, which must regulate national communication markets and enforce local regulations on information, broadcasting, and proprietary rights.

The involvement of government is therefore heavily criticized, even when its intentions are clearly to sponsor public good in the ICT sector. The story of the penetration of global technology corporations into Costa Rica exemplifies the dangers associated with governmental intervention in sectoral buildup.[11] In the period between 1997 and 1999, Costa Rica lost its "banana republic" status and was redubbed "Silicon Valley South": in 1997 Intel Corporation opened a local microprocessor assembly plant with an investment of US$300 million. Intel revenue alone accounted for half of Costa Rican GDP growth for the second half of the 1990s. Intel was courted to launch this plant by local authorities, under the solicitation of the private sector consortium Coalicion Costarricense de Iniciativas de Desarrollo (CINDE), and the Costa Rican government invested heavily in infrastructure and education to make Costa Rica attractive for Intel and a few other technology corporations that followed. The government constructed roads, ran phone lines, upgraded the electricity grid—all in the effort to prepare the ground for titanic foreign direct investment. At the same time, though, Costa Rica was made vulnerable to corporate decisions made in far-away Silicon Valley (North!) headquarters. In this sense, state investments in ICT buildup spill out into private sector profits. The intense privatization of the technology investment broke the ownership link between state and technology. Even if the seeds of today's Internet were planted by ARPA/DARPA and sponsored by the U.S. government, and even if substantial Costa Rican public funds subsidized Intel's foreign direct investment, most technology R&D worldwide is now sponsored (and owned) by venture capital. And the globalization of markets led to capital becoming transnational, drawing on the resources of different nations.

Overall, we see intense involvement of national authorities in the globalization of ICT: states sponsor digital literacy programs, encourage entry of IT corporations into local markets, and fund local infrastructure projects. So while IT seemed initially to be spawned by the private sector, with IT corporations spreading their operations into the emerging market economies, later concerted efforts to close the digital divide emerged primarily through the public sector. In this sense, and in spite of the dire predictions about the "end of history" due to globalization and transnationality, the nation-state seems to be alive and well. As Monroe Price argues, in his work on the state in the age of media, the state has merely redefined its mode of practice of authority to conform to the globalization of ICT.[12] Discussions of technology globalization therefore join the recent social studies debate on the power of the state in the age of globalization.

Technology and National Sovereignty

In spite of the intense work of states to encourage the diffusion of ICTs, transnationality in general and ICT in particular challenge the sovereignty of the nation-state. So although we see intense involvement of individual states in ICT globalization, states have been challenged to respond to several transnational pressures. The attack of globalization on the nation-state, which spurred scholarly discussions about the future of the state in the

age of globalization, comes from two directions: the market and world society.

The most intense pressures toward transnationality come from the intensifying global economy. With world trade reaching new peaks and with the intense mobility of commodities, people, and capital, nation-states are having to confront the issues that emerge from porous borders. The age of ICT coincides with the era of neoliberal models of governance, trade, and finance. "Washington consensus"[13] themes (and pressures) toward deregulation and liberalization inherently weaken the place of the state in setting the social agenda and magnifying the role of multinational corporations. They also work to homogenize national arrangements across national settings. On a technical level alone, these initiatives call for standardization of procedures across borders—in accounting and legal measures, for example—to harmonize global transactions. In this standardization, ICT is crucial. It supplies the means for quick, routine, and formatted exchanges. The e-economy's strengthening regional, or "global city," development creates a distance between development and a nation: technology hubs (see Chapter 2) concentrate e-commerce activity around them, rather than diffuse activity across the nation, and bypass national boundaries. Therefore, conceptually as well as strategically, the e-economy specifically contributes to the condensation of time and space that establishes the "neutralization of place and distance through telematics."[14]

The second source of challenge to the nation-state is from the rapidly growing world society. The work of international organizations in which most ICT decisions are made and initiatives are taken (see previous section) concentrates on global social issues and on global social initiatives, again bypassing state authority in making national policies on ICT and the global digital divide. International organizations exert isomorphic pressures on nation-states by offering similar recommendations to all countries for upgrading ICT infrastructure, investing in computer literacy programs, and encouraging foreign direct investment from technology multinational corporations. In addition, global civil society organizations exert normative pressures toward a resolution of social problems, at the same time enforcing a standard definition of social problems: the global digital divide is seen as a challenge to notions of universal justice and progress ideals that disregard nation-specific heritages of inequality or culture-specific features.

On both fronts—market and world society—ICT challenges state sovereignty. The growing penetration of the world market and the growing authority of transnational nonstate actors to define and prescribe social notions affect the perception of the state as a thriving player in policy making, even at its own national level. Thus, whereas traditional notions of state sovereignty regarded the state as an independent and rational player in international affairs with full command of its unique policy making, the porous nature of national boundaries—physical and conceptual—in the age of globalization provokes states to reformulate sovereignty. ICT has a unique place in the process of reformulating national sovereignty. On the one hand, ICT dramatizes the permeable nature of national boundaries (for example, by allowing flows of information to bypass national censorship and enabling greater penetration of trade flows); on the other hand, ICT reifies notions of sovereignty by calling on the nation-state as a locale for identity and authority (for example, Internet identification embeds the country affiliation for all but the United States, thus reinforcing national location in an age of transnational, or placeless, technology and reinforcing American hegemony by concealing its placelessness as worldliness and leaving the assignment of "localness" in the hands of state authorities).

The discussion of state authority as changing under pressures of globalization, although central to understanding international affairs and to tracing globalization trends, is less emphasized in the work on the global digital divide. Still, with pressure mounting for policy initiatives to close the divide, the state is often called on, even if by transnational players, to address this social problem. State sovereignty, if weakened in the areas of trade and finance, is still alive and well, if changed, in the area of social policy making.

Notes

1. International Telecommunication Union (2003), *World Telecommunication Development Report: Access Indicators for the Information Society* (Geneva: ITU), p. 15.
2. Jennifer Hillner (2000), "Venture Capitals," *Wired*, August 7. Available at www.wired.com.
3. See Xiaowei Luo (2000), "The Rise of the Social Development Model: Institutional Construction of International Technology Organizations, 1856–1993," *International Studies Quarterly* 44(1): 147–175.
4. See Jens Bertelson (2000), "Three Concepts of Globalization," *International Sociology* 15(2): 180–196.

5. Refer to Xiowei Luo (2000), note 3.

6. Refer to Chapter 1 for a review of the historical progression of the technology.

7. John Boli and George Thomas (1999), *Constructing World Culture: International Nongovernmental Organizations since 1875* (Stanford, CA: Stanford University Press), pp. 42–44.

8. For a consideration of the notion of global corporatism, see Marina Ottaway (2001), "Corporatism Goes Global: International Organizations, Nongovernmental Organization Networks, and Transnational Business," *Global Governance* 7(3): 265–292.

9. See Martha Finnemore (1993), "International Organizations as Teachers of Norms: The United Nations Educational, Scientific, and Cultural Organization and Science Policy," *International Organization* 47: 567–597; Martha Finnemore (1996), *National Interests in International Society* (Ithaca, NY: Cornell University Press).

10. See Henry Etzkowitz and Loet Leydesdroff (1997), *U.S. and the Global Knowledge Economy: A Triple Helix of University-Industry-Government Relations* (New York: Pinter).

11. See Megan Kendall (2001), "A Whale in a Swimming Pool," unpublished honors thesis, International Relations Program, Stanford University.

12. Monroe E. Price (2002), *Media and Sovereignty: The Global Media Revolution and Its Challenges to State Power* (Cambridge, MA: MIT Press).

13. "Washington consensus" is the label given to the approach to development that is shared by the international financial institutions that are headquartered in Washington, D.C., such as the International Monetary Fund (IMF) and the World Bank. The consensus identifies the following as the foundations for development: trade and financial liberalization, privatization, deregulation, public expenditure, contraction, and securing of property rights.

14. Saskia Sassen (2001), *The Global City: New York, London, Tokyo* (Princeton, NJ: Princeton University Press), p. 35.

8

Bridging the Divide

Making a Case for Policy

Considering the depth of the global digital divide, is it realistic to expect that it can be bridged? Considering the multiple social issues folded into the technological divide, is it realistic to expect a comprehensive solution? Indeed it is, I argue. As much as the closing of this global gap seems like an impossible task, global ICT diffusion can and should be guided by calculated policy. And just as other issues of access to social resources (such as education and health) are being addressed by social policies, so can the global digital divide be taken up by policy makers. Since I adopt the prism of inequality for examining this social problem, the required policy sets its goal of bridging the digital divide by targeting weak populations: minorities, immigrants, the poor in core countries, and the citizens of developing countries.

"Trends are not destiny," wrote Allen L. Hammond, founder and director of the Digital Dividend project, suggesting that current conditions call for policy planning.[1] Indeed, without guided intervention aimed at closing the global digital divide, it could take generations for the divide to close at its own pace, if ever. Why so long, considering that the "normalization thesis" predicts that the closing of social gaps is imminent? The cause would be the nature of global differences: current rates of expansion of access (or closing of gaps) are coupled with current rates of access and utilization; there is a *multiplicative effect*. The average Internet penetration rate in developed countries in 2001 was 30% per year, while in developing countries the comparable rate was only one tenth of that: about 3% per year. This rate is the multiplier for current conditions. Considering how far behind the developing world is lagging in access and utilization of ICT, the slower rate of its technological expansion dooms it to perpetually lagging behind. At this rate, by the time the global periphery catches up, the technology frontier will be far beyond it: by the time peripheral populations and marginalized populations are using today's ICT, the global elite will be relying on the future cutting-edge technologies. So while existing social inequalities deter people from fully accessing and utilizing ICT, the inequalities may increase the more ICT becomes the marker of social integration and mobility. With "technological literacy" becoming the new criterion for job placement, income, civic engagement, and social prospects, equal distribution of ICT is becoming a critical factor in social planning.

The prospect of doom can be avoided, or at least escaped to some degree. With guided and concerted efforts, digital divides could turn into "digital dividends"; digital gaps could be converted into digital skills that will bear fruit in terms of economic and political progress. With a new, innovative, and multisectoral development strategy that relies on ICT, progress on bridging the current gaps is possible.

In some policy discussions of the global digital divide, the core questions seems to be: To tech or not to tech? In other words, with the cultural invasiveness of ICT, should countries make concerted efforts to upgrade their technological capacities and the digital skills of their citizens or should governments maintain current technologies and not surrender to the technology race? In an age of market logic and competitive edge, must all countries master the same cutting-edge digital technology?

This dilemma is clearly voiced by neo-Luddites, who fear technological change and the dramatic and still unforeseen impacts it may have on human life (Box 8.1). Their objections to technological change are relevant to the issue of the digital divide; neo-Luddites raise such questions as Is digital Luddism an option for people today? If digital technology is to be mastered, what sort of digital technologies are relevant for comprehensive, or holistic, social progress? And most important, can technology be a solution to all human and social problems?[2]

The global digital divide is intertwined with other social problems worldwide: social inequality and injustice, economic and political conditions, immigration, resources, and on and on. To solve the global digital divide is, then, to also chip away at other social problems; social policies to remedy inequalities in access to and use of digital technology are interconnected with social policies to resolve these ills. This task is immense. Prudent, thoughtful, and effective policy should emerge from an analysis of the root causes of the targeted social ill. Steps toward policy making to resolve the problem of the global digital divide are already being taken.

Box 8.1

Luddites and Neo-Luddites

Worker riots in the wool industry, which started in 1811 in Nottinghamshire, spread to the whole of England in the following five years. The wool industry's workers were led by General Ned Ludd, whose name was used to title the movement as the "Luddite movement" and the disturbances as the "Luddite riots." The workers expressed their distress over worsening working conditions, extensive wage reductions, and massive unemployment by smashing the recently incorporated spinning and weaving machines (then called "frames") that, in the era of the Industrial Revolution, were replacements for workers' labor in mass production. As a response to the riots, the British government ordered some 12,000 troops to curb the violence, and the Frame Breaking Act of 1812 declared machine breaking as a capital offense punishable by death. The riots, which were seen by the government as mob-led political subversion that gravely affected British industrialization, symbolized the opposition to social change that results from technological advancement.

The violence of the nineteenth century's Luddites against technology should not be conflated with hostility toward technology per se; rather, the workers' grievance was against working conditions and the machines were merely the easy targets for their rage. However, the term "Luddism" has been used ever since to denote opposition to social changes created by technological change. Luddism came to mean the resistance to technology-driven social change and the raising of moral and ethical objections to technological modernization.

Neo-Luddites oppose today's technological changes that create new social arrangements. To some, yesterday's weaving machines are today's computers and cellular phones. In the words of Kirkpatrick Sale, the leader of the neo-Luddites, "We modern-day Luddites are not, or at least not yet, taking up the sledgehammer and the torch and gun to resist the new machinery, but rather taking up the book and the lecture and organizing people to raise these issues. . . . It was astonishing how good [smashing a computer] made me feel! . . . It was a statement. . . . And remarkably satisfying when it is injurious to property, not people."*

As the Liberty lads o'er the sea
Bought their freedom, and cheaply, with blood,
So we, boys, we
Will die fighting, or live free,
And down with all kings but King Ludd!

—Lord Byron, *Song for the Luddites,* 1816

---

*Kirkpatrick Sale (1995, June), interview in *Wired* 3(6).

Proudly, African policy makers demonstrate that in anticipation of the World Summit on Information Society (WSIS) 2003 and 2005 meetings, many African governments developed explicit ICT policies and plans.[3] But policy should not be drafted for policy's sake. In the following section, I contemplate the various sources or causes of the global digital divide so that we can later assess policies to remedy it.

Sources of the Global Digital Divide

Understanding the causes of global technology-based inequality is the basis of conceiving of possible solutions to this social problem. Let me pause for a short sociological detour into the foundations of the digital divide and its global parameters. In this section I invoke common sociological explanations of social inequality and apply them to the issue of the global digital divide (Box 8.2).

Because of the nature of the global digital divide—its multidimensionality and its scope—its sources spring from diverse social spheres, from cultural traditions and individual preferences to structural social conditions. Sociological approaches vary along these lines, too, from theories that emphasize the role of the individual in the social process to theories that focus on structural social conditions, from theories that analyze the interactions among people to theories that perceive environmental circumstances as prime. In general, sociological attention is given to the "stratification system"—the institutional setting of social inequalities along lines of prized social resources. Key to understanding the stratification system are (1) the definitions of certain social goods as valuable and desirable, thus creating the normative foundation for stratification, (2) the allocation of social goods across social groups, thus establishing distributional rules for social positions and classes and for uneven division of the prized social resources, and (3) the dynamics and historical change in the definitions and rules, thus opening up the possibility for mobility and its mechanisms. To explain social stratification, many think of it in terms of functions and dysfunctions (how the match of rewards to capacity serves to satisfy social needs); others focus on power and mechanisms of coercion (how control and pressure maintain the status quo of power differentials).

In the study of social stratification, two notions are particularly important when considering social inequalities specific to the age of high technology. The first issue concerns the dynamic nature of social inequalities and is commonly referred to as the "Matthew effect" (Box 8.3).

Box 8.2
Explaining Disparities in Access and Participation

Individual factors
Self-perception (and choice of role models)
Acquired skills and training
Future opportunities

Organizational factors
Science, math, and technical curricula in schools and universities
Teaching methods
Educational infrastructure and resources
Market (labor and production) infrastructure and resources

Societal factors
Family and peers
Cultural traditions
Societal attitudes
Class distinction and criteria
Regulatory framework
Political regime

World factors
Initiatives and intervention of international organizations
Political and economic alliances
Cultural boundaries

(Adapted from categorization by Christine Min Wotipka.)

The implication of the Matthew effect for knowledge-based initiatives for development is that at times the efforts may feel like swimming against the current: the tendency toward perpetuation of social inequalities, if it does not deepen them, may delay efforts to close social gaps. The other issue is the duration of innovation and change: knowledge-based development is a long-term process, thus requiring long-term social commitment to its solution. Not only has the international community been fighting poverty and underdevelopment for decades without alleviating these problems altogether, but private sector ICT initiatives require great patience and persistence. ICT R&D periods proceeding each remarkable achievement are decidedly long. For example, the 1983 event of Motorola starting commercial operation of its DynaTAC cellular system was preceded by 15 years and $100 million committed by Motorola to the development of its cellular program. And the processes of commercial R&D did not stop in 1983. The implication of the duration element is that persistence is a requirement.

Box 8.3

The Matthew Effect and the Digital Divide

For unto every one that hath shall be given, and he shall have abundance: but from him that hath not shall be taken away even that which he hath.

—Matthew 15:292

The principle of unequal sharing and accumulation of social resources that is described in the Gospel of Matthew is still used these days to express the pervasive and dynamic nature of social inequality. This passage communicates the notion of change in social gaps: social divides tend to expand, distancing further and further apart poor from rich, educated from uneducated, socially connected from marginalized. In this sense, the Matthew effect describes not only how the rich get richer (in any sort of social resource) but also how the poor get poorer (again, in any sort of social resource). As Lester Thurow describes it, "Once wealth is accumulated, the opportunity to make more money multiplies since accumulated wealth leads to income-earning opportunities that are not open to those without wealth."*

This sage proclamation opens a philosophical debate on the nature of social inequality: Should this statement be taken to mean that inequality and gaping social divides are an inevitable condition of human life? Or is this statement to be interpreted as hopeful, that those who are fortunate enough to have social resources can, with their labor and ambition, add to their fortunes, while those who waste their resources, great or small, are doomed to further waste? Either way, it is an astute description of current conditions in access to education, in scientific recognition and rewards, and in monetary funds.

How does the Matthew effect relate to the digital divide? The same principle of gaping social divides applies to technological divides. Those who have access to digital technology and are accustomed to use it are more likely to continue upgrading their skills and their digital gadgets over time; those who do not access or use cutting-edge technology are missing the opportunity ever to integrate into fast-changing modern society and are thus falling behind. Technology is, then, one of those social resources that differentiate people, perpetuate the differentiations, and characterize life trajectories.

*Lester Thurow (1996), *The Future of Capitalism: How Today's Economic Forces Shape Tomorrow's World* (New York: Morrow), p. 243.

What Sort of Problem Is the Problem of the Global Digital Divide?

I previously emphasized the two core dimensions of the problem of the global digital divide: access (the opportunity of contact with the technology) and use (utilization of the technology once accessed). I discuss this problem through a social prism: most of the factors I mention as sources of inequality in access and use are social, as are the targets of the programs and initiatives I highlight. But could the problem of the global digital divide be a problem of technology (and its diffusion) rather than a problem of social divides and inequality?

Certainly some dimensions of the problem (and of its possible solutions) are technological: Can signal reception be magnified to reach faraway rural areas of the country? Can the price be lowered to allow widespread purchase of the technology? Can the technology rely on local language or sign-based interface to allow access to non-English speakers or to illiterate people? These matters are in the hands of the tech people, the experts who have the skills to develop the technology toward unmediated access and wide use. They are also, to a great degree, in the hands of people who sponsor technological advances in either the private or the public sectors because they provide the incentive and sponsorship for the costly and long R&D process. Clearly, technological advances exemplified in such initiatives as the Simputer or UNESCO's radio distribution in rural Africa may not be enough to bridge the global digital divide.

In spite of these technological components of the global digital divide, there are several indications that the divide is primarily a social matter. Specifically, the problem—its definition and the guidance toward its solution—is in the hands of social actors, from governments and corporations to civil society organizations. And most important, the close correspondence between digital divides and social markers (such as age, race, and gender) reveals that technological inequalities are primarily another layer of social inequalities.

The question of whether the problem of the global digital divide is technological or social is not an abstract or a theoretical question; rather, it goes to the heart of the causes and to the possible solutions. The definition of the global digital divide as one or another sort of problem charts the path of policy: if it is a problem of technology, then its solution lies in technological upgrades, whereas if it is a social problem, then its solution rests with empowerment and human development initiatives. And furthermore, if the global digital divide is specifically a matter of social inequality, then the definition of the global digital divide is further complicated by consideration of what accounts for unjust social inequality. The debate rages between equality of chances or equality of outcomes as the measure of inequality (and of success in curbing it). On the one hand, some argue that by offering equal chances or opportunities, we level the social plain to encourage fair and just distribution of social resources; on the other hand, others argue that just and fair distribution can be judged only by outcomes or results of social initiatives to produce the desired equality.

Figure 8.1

Dimensions of the Problem of the Global Digital Divide

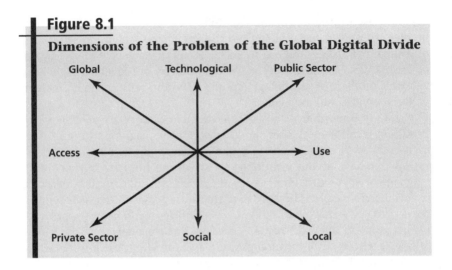

In summary, the problem of the global digital divide is made ever more complex by the multiplicity of approaches to social inequality, in addition to the multiplicity of approaches to the specific issue of the global digital divide. In Figure 8.1 I chart a few of the debates raging on these issues, revealing the tensions between a series of matters: Is the global digital divide a global problem or a national and local matter of action? Is its solution in the hands of the public and government sector or in the hands of the much richer but also more self-interested and profit-motivated private sector? And is the global digital divide a technological or a social problem? Although the debates construct these tensions as dichotomous, most debates revolve around the matter of balance or proportion. For example, no one is arguing that only the private sector should guide and sponsor the bridging of the global digital divide. Rather, we must call for cooperation between the private and the public sectors in offering solutions for this social problem, making the debate, if any, revolve around which of the sectors should take which role (leader or sponsor) and to what degree (primary or secondary).

What Is Being Done Already?

There are as many different approaches to the problem of the global digital divide as there are initiatives that reflect each approach. Therefore, the "map" of current projects to bridge the global digital divide mirrors the various emphases: access or use, technological or social, private sector or public sector. The various strategies, many of which are already being used to deal with the global digital divide worldwide, can be categorized by their sponsors (private sector or public sector, government sources or civil society) and by their target population (disenfranchised populations, industry, education, and others). These programs and initiatives can also be classified by their goals: empowerment or developmental leapfrogging. Even though there are so many crosscutting classifications, I here highlight only a few noteworthy global initiatives to curb the global digital divide. Much like the programs of the Millennium Development Goals (Chapter 5), most of these initiatives are not sufficiently mature to be subject to thorough evaluation, and their successes are currently anecdotal. Still, they chart for us a path of possibilities for the solution to the problem of the global digital divide.

Most initial programs tackle the issue of access to ICT by building infrastructure for digital access, in the hope of skipping steps in technological development to expedite technological and economic progress. In Cambodia, by 2002, 90% of phones were cellular, thus practically skipping the land-line version of phone technology and enabling a more rapid absorption and more extensive utilization of cutting-edge phone technology. Similarly, Malaysian authorities installed satellite communication in rural areas to overcome the shortage of land-line communications and the slow diffusion of Internet connections. Satellite and cellular shortcuts like these two are cost-effective solutions for establishing a network among a large number of locales spread across geographically dispersed areas.

Providing public access opportunities further addresses the issue of access to ICT. As a solution, Intel Corporation initiated the Clubhouse Network to help American youth from urban and poor backgrounds to develop computer skills. The network offers free computer and Internet workshops in after-school facilities; specifically, one of the Clubhouse Network programs engages enrolled youth by encouraging them to create both software and hardware for computer games. Public access is therefore available through public venues (community centers, libraries, and schools), as well as through private entrepreneurial routes (cybercafés and businesses after-hours arrangements). In these ways, access solutions are emerging through small-scale entrepreneurial initiatives as well as through corporate social responsibility venues and government paths.

It seems, however, that public-funded access may be crucial in developing countries and in poor communities. This point becomes clear through the comparison of public access Internet use in China and the United States. In the United States, only some 4% of Internet users access the Internet through public venues; in China some 25% of Internet users are students who go on-line at their school's computer labs. In poor communities there are not sufficient available earnings to allow for such consumption of information and communications. Obviously, then, issues of funding R&D projects are far beyond the reach of small and impoverished communities; most R&D funding is drawn from governmental expenditure on ICT projects or from corporate investments and corporate social responsibility budgets.

Last, to coordinate such different initiatives and to chart policies, many countries turn to revising ministerial duties to accommodate ICT needs. Countries like China and South Korea advance national ICT interests through concerted governmental efforts, which are coordinated at the ministerial level. Under ministerial supervision and guidance, public works projects to enhance ICT infrastructure and access are moving forward. The South Korean Ministry of Communication and Information launched the Korea Information Infrastructure plan to offer a private-sector-backed network of broadband communication throughout the land, and it established the Ministry of Information Industry in 1998 by recasting the duties of the old Korean Ministry of Electronic Industry and Ministry of Post and Telecommunications into a new proactive format.

A second strategic path for tackling specifically the problem of utilization of digital technology is to stimulate technology creation and demand. Stimulation is offered through educational and training programs, primarily in schools. And again, private sector initiatives are key to educational agendas. For example, Cisco set up some 10,000 Cisco Networking Academies in over 145 countries and in all 50 U.S. states. Working closely with UNDP, the World Bank Group, and local governments, Cisco provides training in Internet technology and networking, as well as training of local instructors and teachers to carry on the mission. Through Cisco's academies, locals are certified in several IT-related professions and helped with job placement.[4] Similarly, Coca-Cola launched an e-learning initiative in different countries, sponsoring educational technology programs in cooperation with local activists and government officials.[5] In the Philippines, for example, Coca-Cola works with the Foundation for Information Technology Education and Development (FIT-ED), a local nongovernmental organization, to formulate IT education programs in local schools, to establish IT centers for educational purposes in various locations, and to train local teachers and education administrators in future teaching of these skills.

In this way, Coca-Cola, Cisco, and other multinational corporations tackle the problem of ICT-related resources and skills in the primary- and secondary-education sectors, while also providing a wedge into workforce changes. Private sector initiatives come mostly from corporate social responsibility budgets, and the corporations battle any accusation that their charity work is masking a strategic move toward creating market dependencies: "Doing good and doing well are not mutually exclusive," says Anand Tawker, the head of Hewlett-Packard's e-inclusion initiative in Asia, about his company's "blended strategy" to combine philanthropic efforts with corporate for-profit aims.[6] Can developing countries, marginalized populations, and emerging regions be a profit-generating sector for these IT multinationals? Some cynically regard social responsibility initiatives by IT multinationals as a response to the saturation of their traditional markets and a search for new consumer sectors. Indeed, the sheer size of the developing world may sustain the profitability of the IT sector, even if at smaller profit margins. But profit consideration may not be in contradiction to the social results of upgrading technological access and utilization in these marginalized segments of the world population.

Because the private sector in most developing countries is small and weak, corporations in developing countries have remained relatively mute on IT initiatives. Unlike global corporations with abundant charity budgets and sometimes social image problems they are trying to solve, local businesses mostly take a small role in long-term socially oriented projects. This bias toward sponsorship from Western corporations is interpreted by many to be yet more evidence of the perpetuation of Western domination in technology and aid in particular and in social initiatives in general.

Much of the resolution of the problems of ICT use relies on increasing the public's awareness of ICT potential. Awareness may emerge from fostering community engagement in technology planning through education of communities about the potential and risks in ICT penetration. This course of action is not merely an empowerment strategy; rather, it makes the public into a decisive partner in governance decisions. The strategy to increase ICT use, although ICT use is desired, is problematic in societies that have no tradition of civic empowerment and engagement.

Last, strategies to bridge the global digital divide may focus on the social inequalities that compound the digital divide. Since variations in digital access among countries are obviously related to income differentials, they may be addressed through a country's social welfare policy in state initiatives to expand access by making PCs and the Internet available at public libraries and community centers, in educational policies to expand digital literacy and to facilitate access, and in economic policies to encourage reduction in connection costs.[7]

Overall, various strategies have been implemented to bridge the digital divide, both globally and nationally, from East Asian educational reforms and African telecommunication policies to Indian diaspora recruiting initiatives and Israeli R&D sponsorship strategies. Different countries form different policies and have different rates of success, yet lessons can be learned from the variety and conditions of the reforms. Unfortunately, to date, most policies to bridge the digital divide have fallen short of expectations: the digital divide, globally and nationally, is still thriving. This failure may stem from the scope of the policies drafted. As Pipa Norris and colleagues argue, "The policy fixes are too specific, the problem of social inequalities—too endemic."[8] What, then, needs to be done to bridge the global digital divide? What new and innovative policies should be drafted to remedy this pervasive social condition?

Beyond Connectivity

The complexity and social embeddedness of the problem of the global digital divide suggest the need for a tight interdependence among policies of education, migration, technology, economics, aid, intellectual property regulation, and so on. It is not solely ICT that will solve gaps in development, and the solution for the global digital divide will not come solely from technology policies.[9] Much as its title suggests, the problem of the global digital divide includes social, technological, and global dimensions. Policies that address the global digital divide, therefore, need to be comprehensive ones, paying attention to the variety of dimensions that shape human conditions. In this sense, I am making a case for literacy, creativity, and appropriateness.

Cooperative efforts among the private sector, governments, and civil society organizations pay attention to multiple social dimensions of the problems that have a chance of ever closing these gaps. The market or private sector alone cannot solve the problem of the digital divide, because the problem extends beyond matters of access and affordability. Neither can the public sector alone address this problem. The increasing demand for all kinds of policies, especially in developing countries, is overwhelming government officials, national budgets, and local capacity. The complexity of the problem calls, therefore, for comprehensive, cross-sector cooperation. With all-inclusive and wide-scoped policies, we will enable the much hoped-for leapfrogging into the digital future.

In her opening address to the first TechNation Summit, held in San Francisco in September 2004, TechNation's host and leader, Dr. Moira Gunn, referred to the words of Peter Schwartz, the cofounder of the Global Business Network. Schwartz maintains that 92% of all scientists throughout human history are alive today, as are 85% of all engineers. This, said Gunn, is inspiring evidence that "the great tsunami wave of technology is still ahead of us." Indeed, the great impact of technology on humanity and its potential is still in our future. We therefore must manage technology, guide its uses, and apply them toward human welfare.

Notes

1. Allen L. Hammond (2001), "Digitally Empowered Development, *Foreign Affairs* 80(2). Available at www.foreignaffairs.org/2001/2.
2. A most eloquent and prolific defender of neo-Luddism is David Noble. To read further on the arguments, see David F. Noble (1993), *Progress without People: In Defense of Luddism* (Chicago: Kerr); David F. Noble (2002), *Digital Diploma Mills: The Automation of Higher Education* (New York: Monthly Review Press).
3. Aida Opoku-Mensah (2004), "Twin Peaks: WSIS from Geneva to Tunis," *Gazette* 66(3–4): 256.
4. To learn more about the Cisco academies, access http://cisco.netacad. net/public/academy/About.html.
5. See http://www2.coca-cola.com/citizenship/education.html.
6. Cited in "Beyond the Digital Divide" (2004, March 13), *Economist Technology Quarterly*, p. 8.
7. See Pipa Norris, W. Lance Bennett, and Robert M. Entman (2001), *Digital Divide: Civic Engagement, Information Poverty, and the Internet Worldwide* (Cambridge, UK: Cambridge University Press), p. 79.
8. Ibid., p. 91.
9. See, for example, the expression of the same sentiment in the various contributions to Bart Cammaerts, Leo Van Audenhove, Gert Nulens, and Caroline Pauwels (eds.) (2004), *Beyond the Digital Divide: Reducing Exclusion, Fostering Inclusion* (Brussels: Brussels University Press).

Appendix:
Chronology of the Computer Age

This short timeline of the field of digital technology marks the birthdates of gadgets, languages, and patents. It is, thus, a "mixed bag" of events: advances in material engineering and thus the making of chips is complemented by experimentation with networking and with audio and visual transmissions; advances in software and hardware occur in parallel; all are solidified by the dramatic buildup of the corporate high-tech field and venture capital. This timeline is, therefore, a heavily abbreviated history of the field.

1945

Vanneavar Bush, in an article in the July issue of the *Atlantic Monthly*, imagines a personal computer and names it "memex."

1946

ENIAC, the first computer, designed by John Mauchly and J. Presper Eckert with a speed of 5,000 operations per second, is displayed to the public.

1947

William Shockley, Walter Brattain, and John Bardeen, scientists at Bell Telephone Laboratories, showcase their new invention, the "transistor" (short for "transfer resistance"), or point-contact transistor amplifier, which eventually replaces the vacuum tubes that were used on computers at the time.

Sources: Ken Polsson (2003), "Chronology of Personal Computers," available at http://www.islandnet.com/~kpolsson/comphist/, accessed April 4, 2003, updated August 30, 2004; Computer History Museum, Mountain View, California, available at http://www.computerhistory.org/timeline/, accessed April 4, 2003; Steven E. Schoenherr's chronology of the computer age at http://history.acusd.edu/gen/recording/computer1.html, accessed September 3, 2004; Martin Kenney (2003), "The Growth and Development of the Internet in the United States," in Bruce Kogut (ed.), *The Global Internet Economy* (Cambridge, MA: MIT Press), pp. 69–108.

1948

Claude Shannon, in "The Mathematical Theory of Communication," describes how to code data to check for accuracy of computer transmission and also identifies the bit as the fundamental unit of data and, coincidentally, the basic unit of computation.

1949

Maurice Wilkes assembles the EDSAC, the first practical stored-program computer, at Cambridge University and establishes a library of short programs called subroutines stored on punched paper tapes.

1950

The National Bureau of Standards constructs the SEAC (Standards Eastern Automatic Computer) in Washington as a laboratory for testing components and systems for setting computer standards.

1951

UNIVAC, or ERA 1101, which was commissioned by the U.S. Navy and built by Engineering Research Associates of Minneapolis, is the first commercially produced computer. The UNIVAC-I is delivered to its first customer, the U.S. Census Bureau, with a price tag of more than $1 million each.

1952

Under a contractual obligation to share its design with other research institutes, Princeton's Institute for Advanced Studies permits John von Neumann's IAS computer to be cloned: the MANIAC at Los Alamos Scientific Laboratory, the ILLIAC at the University of Illinois, the Johnniac at Rand Corporation, the SILLIAC in Australia, and others are built on the same blueprint.

1953

IBM ships its first electronic computer, the 701; 19 machines are sold in the first three years of production.

1954

Gordon Teal of Texas Instruments Inc. develops the silicon-based junction transistor and lowers its price to $2.50, thus launching TI's days in radio manufacturing.

1955

AT&T Bell Laboratories' TRADIC, the first fully transistorized computer, is launched; it occupies only 3 cubic feet.

First meeting of SHARE, the IBM users group, convenes, marking the consolidation of user groups as a relevant stakeholder.

The March 28 cover of *Time* magazine features Tom Watson Jr., the president of IBM, with the cover story devoted to the "brain builders," referring to the IMB 702 model, nicknamed the "giant brain."

1956

IBM introduces the RAMAC 305, the first hard drive, with 50 platters 2 feet in diameter and with a total capacity of 5 MB. It takes another 15 years for the first hard drives for PCs to appear, also initially with a capacity of around 5 MB.

1957

FORTRAN (short for FORmula TRANslator), a new computer language, is launched, enabling computers to perform a repetitive task from a single set of instructions by using loops.

1958

Japan's NEC builds the country's first electronic computer, the NEAC-1101.

Jack Kilby creates the first integrated circuit at Texas Instruments, proving that resistors and capacitors could exist on the same piece of semiconductor material.

1959

IBM's 7000 series mainframes become the company's first transistorized computers. The "Stretch" or 7030, the top of this line, features a 64-bit expression and is the first computer to be considered in terms of "architecture."

1960

Digital Equipment introduces the first minicomputer equipped with a keyboard and monitor, the PDP-1, for US$120,000.

COBOL (COmmon Business-Oriented Language) is developed by a team drawn from several computer manufacturers and the Pentagon.

1963

Douglas Engelbart invents the "mouse" pointing device for computers.

ASCII (American Standard Code for Information Interchange) is developed to permit machines from different manufacturers to exchange data.

In the robotics field, the Rancho Arm, designed with six joints to simulate the flexibility of a human arm and controlled by a computer, is acquired by Stanford University's medical center.

1964

BASIC (Beginners All-purpose Symbolic Instruction Code) is developed by John Kemeny at Dartmouth College.

The American Standards Association adopts ASCII as a standard code for data transfer.

AT&T unveils the picturephone, or "see as you talk" phone, which plants the seed for future digitized picture communication.

1966

John van Geen, of the Stanford Research Institute, perfects the acoustically coupled modem to distinguish data from background noise heard over long-distance phone lines.

The HP-2115, Hewlett-Packard's first general-purpose computer, becomes available.

1967

Medtronics constructs the first internal pacemaker using integrated circuits.

1968

Douglas C. Engelbart, of the Stanford Research Institute, demonstrates the integrated PC: a system combining a keyboard, keypad, mouse, and windows, demonstrating the use of a word processor, a hypertext system, and remote collaborative work with colleagues.

The Apollo Guidance Computer makes its debut orbiting the Earth on *Apollo 7,* launching a NASA use of computerized guidance and communication tasks.

1969

Honeywell starts selling its H316 "Kitchen Computer," the first home computer, in the Neiman Marcus catalogue, priced at US$10,600.

IBM builds SCAMP, one of the world's first personal computers.

Intel announces the 1-kilobit RAM chip.

Kenneth Thompson and Dennis Ritchie, of AT&T Bell Laboratories, develop the UNIX operating system.

Internet servers are installed at University of California Los Angeles, Stanford Research Institute, University of California Santa Barbara, and the University of Utah.

1970

Xerox opens the Palo Alto Research Center (PARC).

The Department of Defense establishes four nodes on the ARPANET: the University of California Santa Barbara, the University of California Los Angeles, SRI International, and the University of Utah.

Citizens and Southern National Bank, in Valdosta, Georgia, installs the country's first automatic teller machine (ATM).

1971

Texas Instruments develops the first microcomputer-on-a-chip, containing over 15,000 transistors.

The Kenback Corporation introduces the Kenback-1 computer, for US$750. It uses a 1-KB MOS memory made by Intel.

Niklaus Wirth invents the Pascal programming language.

An IBM team, originally led by Alan Shugart, invents the 8-inch floppy diskette as a data storage medium.

1972

Brian Kernighan and Dennis Ritchie develop the C programming language. Initially associated solely with UNIX systems, C (and its derivations) would grow to become one of the dominant computer languages.

Steve Wozniak builds his "blue box" as a tone generator to make free phone calls.

ARPANET and its e-mail capability are introduced to the public at the International Computer Communication Conference (ICCC).

158

1973

The Alto workstation computer is turned on at Xerox PARC; its first on-screen image is Cookie Monster of *Sesame Street*.

The Micral, the first computer system referred to as a microcomputer, is introduced, selling for US$1,750.

The TV Typewriter, designed by Don Lancaster, provides the first display of alphanumeric information on an ordinary television set.

1974

Creative Computing, the first magazine for home computer users, is founded.

1975

Telenet, the first commercial packet-switching network and civilian equivalent of ARPANET, is established.

Ed Roberts coins the term "personal computer" as part of an advertising campaign for the Altair; the term "PC" first appears in print in the May 1976 issue of *Byte* magazine.

Bill Gates and Paul Allen license their just-written BASIC, the first computer language program written for a personal computer, to MITS, their first customer.

By June, MITS sales of Altair computers hit US$1 million.

1976

Apple Computer Company is established (on April Fool's Day, April 1) by Steve Wozniak and Steve Jobs, selling its Apple I computer board as a kit for US$666.66.

The Personal Computing Festival, held in Atlantic City, New Jersey, becomes the site of the first computer hobbyist clubs.

"Microsoft" is registered as a trademark.

The Cray I, the first commercially successful vector processor, becomes the fastest machine of its day: 166 million floating-point operations per second.

1977

The Apple II, with its brilliant graphics and colors, comes out and immediately attracts game lovers and designers.

The TRS-80, Tandy Radio Shack's first desktop computer, is sold for US$599.95 and sells some 10,000 units in its first year.

Motorola sets up an experimental cellular phone system, employing both portable and vehicular phones, in the suburbs of Washington, D.C. At the same time, Ericsson installs the first mobile network in Saudi Arabia.

AT&T and GTE install the first wireless fiber-optic communication system.

1978

Texas Instruments Inc. introduces Speak & Spell, a talking learning aid for ages 7 and up. Its debut marks the first electronic duplication of the human voice on a single chip of silicon.

1979

John Shoch and Jon Hupp at Xerox PARC design the computer "worm," intended to provide an efficient testing of a computer's functions.

The first computer modem is introduced by Hayes.

1980

Philips develops the first optical data storage disk, which has 60 times the capacity of a $5^1/_4$-inch floppy disk. This first disk, which stores data through indelible marks burned by a laser, cannot be overwritten.

Apple reaches US$100 million in annual sales and goes public.

1981

The release of MS-DOS (Microsoft Disk Operating System) as the basic software for the newly released IBM PC establishes the long partnership between IBM and Microsoft.

The Osborne I, the first portable computer, weighing 24 pounds and costing $1,795, is released. The machine features a 5-inch display, 64 kilobytes of memory, a modem, and two 5¼-inch floppy disk drives.

Sony starts shipping the first 3½-inch floppy drives and diskettes.

1982

Time magazine declares the computer "Machine of the Year."

Disney releases *Tron*, which relies on computer animation and also features computers and hackers as its main characters.

Hewlett-Packard's adoption of the 3½-inch floppy for general use establishes this format as the industry standard for a microfloppy over other contenders.

Philips upgrades its data storage disk to an erasable optical disk, called a magneto-optic disk.

Apple reaches US$1 billion in annual sales, with 3,000 independent retail outlets worldwide, 1,400 of which are in North America.

1983

The first IBM PC clone, introduced by Compaq Computer Corporation and using the same software as the IBM PC, is launched; Compaq reports first-year sales of $111 million.

Microsoft announces Word and Windows (even though Windows does not ship until 1985).

The Musical Instrument Digital Interface (MIDI), which became the industry standard for commanding music synthesizers, is introduced at the first North American Music Manufacturers show in Los Angeles.

After 15 years and $100 million of development, Motorola's first DynaTAC cellular system begins commercial operation.

1984

The term "cyberspace" is coined in William Gibson's novel *Neuromancer,* which also spawns the "cyberpunk" genre.

Philips and Sony announce the CD-ROM, able to hold 550 megabytes of prerecorded data. A year later, *Grolier's Electronic Encyclopedia* is the first general-interest CD-ROM released on this medium. Its 9 million words take up only 12 percent of the available space.

1985

The launch of PageMaker by Aldus sparks interest in desktop publishing.

DARPA transfers ARPANET to the National Science Foundation, which quickly opens access to all universities worldwide under the condition that they allow access to all qualified users on campus.

NSF decrees that NSFNET sites must use the TCP/IP protocol, so this protocol almost instantaneously becomes the standard for transmission.

1987

IBM introduces its PS/2 machines, which are the first to offer standard packages of 3½-inch floppy disk drive, video graphics, and Intel's 80386 chip. IBM also releases a new operating system, OS/2, at the same time, allowing the use of a mouse with IBM PCs for the first time. By the end of the year, IBM has shipped more than 1 million units.

Apple sells its 1 millionth Macintosh.

HyperCard (a software platform for developing in-home applications) is launched by Apple engineer William Atkinson.

The first U.S. nationwide 100% digital fiber-optic network is completed.

1988

Pixar's *Tin Toy* becomes the first computer-animated film to win an Academy Award.

The first malicious use of the worm is the flooding of ARPANET by 23-year-old Robert Morris, the son of a computer security expert for the National Security Agency.

Apple Computers and Microsoft enter into a long litigation war, suing each other on matters of infringement of rights and violations of contract; HP is also named in suits.

The Open Software Foundation is established.

The bus standard used on IBM AT compatibles is given the name Industry Standard Architecture (ISA).

1989

Maxis releases SimCity, a video game that helps launch of series of simulators.

"Virtual reality," denoting a computer-generated 3-D environment that allows a user to interact with this environment, is introduced by Silicon Graphics and Autodesk at the 1989 Siggraph convention in Boston.

Motorola's MicroTAC personal cellular telephone, the smallest and lightest on the market, is introduced.

The Personal Computer Memory Card International Association (PCMCIA) is formed to develop a memory card standard for personal computers.

The first MacWorld Expo is held, in Boston, Massachusetts.

IBM licenses the NeXTSTEP operating system from NeXT for US$10 million.

To date, there are about 25 million MS-DOS users worldwide; 24% of American homes have PCs; 22 million PCs are in use worldwide; 236,000 CD-ROMs are shipped worldwide during 1989 alone. In market shares, Hewlett-Packard holds 24.2% of the workstation market, DEC 21%; of PC spreadsheet software market shares, Lotus 1-2-3 holds 54%, Borland Quattro 3%, Microsoft Excel 12.6%; of desktop operating systems, OS/2 holds less than 1%, MS-DOS 66%.

1990

HyperText Markup Language (HTML), which became the basic format of the World Wide Web, is introduced by Tim Berners-Lee while at CERN.

Shearson Lehman Hutton produces a forecast of PC advances before the year 2000, predicting a merger between Compaq Computer and Hewlett-Packard in 1995.

Microsoft introduces a Russian version of MS-DOS 4.01 for the Soviet market. It also introduces PowerPoint presentation software for Windows and PowerPoint 2.0 for Windows, the first application to use OLE (object linking and embedding).

Microsoft bashing becomes standard: Pete Peterson, executive vice president of WordPerfect, is quoted as saying that Microsoft is the "fox that takes you across the river and then eats you," and Paul Grayson, cofounder of Micrografx, is quoted as saying that "there is only one person with fewer friends than Saddam Hussein. And that's Bill Gates."

The first CD-ROM magazine is published: *Nautilus*.

Gilbert Hyatt is granted a patent for "a single-chip integrated-circuit computer architecture," 20 years after his first application for the patent.

The North American Commodore User Group Association is formed to support the dwindling number of Commodore users. In spite of its decline, the Commodore 64 of the early 1980s is considered the Model T of personal computers.

1991

The first World Wide Web server and browser become available to the general public.

Go announces its PenPoint operating system for mobile pen-based computers.

In January, Compaq Computer reports its first billion-dollar quarter.

A group of 21 companies creates the Advanced Computing Environment (ACE) initiative to establish a new standard for advanced desktop computers, based on RISC processing. Members include Compaq Computer, Microsoft, and Digital Equipment.

The Business Applications Performance Corporation (BAPCo) is founded to develop sets of benchmarks for testing computer system performance.

AT&T and NCR sign a merger agreement.

In May, the first Web server is introduced at the Stanford Linear Accelerator; by the beginning of 1992, 26 Web servers exist.

By summer, the number of personal computers worldwide running MS-DOS reaches 60 million; Microsoft DOS holds 75% of market share in personal computer-operating systems; Mike Maples, vice president of operating systems and applications at Microsoft, is quoted as saying: "My job is to get a fair share of the software applications market, and that's 100 percent."

In Finland, Linus Torvalds develops Linux, a UNIX operating system variant.

CD-R (Recordable) is introduced for computer use.

In November, IBM exits from the software market.

1992

Tim Berners-Lee founds the W3 Consortium to coordinate the development of the World Wide Web.

In January, Microsoft stock reaches US$113/share, making Bill Gates the richest man in the United States, at US$6.4 billion.

At COMDEX/Spring '92, held in Chicago, Microsoft begins to ship Windows 3.1 and ships 10 million copies within the first four months. The software comprises over 3 million lines of code.

WordPerfect holds 71% of U.S. market share in word processor software.

ISO 10646 is passed by member countries, providing a standard 32-bit character set of all known characters and symbols.

Fortune magazine inducts Steve Jobs into its National Business Hall of Fame.

Intel announces that the name "Pentium" has been chosen for its next processor, currently referred to as P5; Jerry Sanders, chairman of Advanced Micro Devices, is quoted as saying that the name is the perfect "name for toothpaste."

Fall COMDEX, held in Las Vegas, brings together about 2,000 company booths and 145,000 people.

1993

Mosaic, the first popular graphic interface to the WWW, is introduced.

PalmPilot is marketed, launching a market for sophisticated handheld computing devices.

Sprint launches two major high-speed components of the "information superhighway": it is the first U.S. carrier to offer asynchronous transfer mode (ATM) service and the first to announce plans for a nationwide synchronous optical network (SONET).

In February, the Federal Trade Commission holds the first in a series of votes on whether to charge Microsoft with unfair trade practices; the vote is a tie. In July the FTC decides to drop consideration of similar charges against Intel. In August, while the FTC decides not to pursue the case against Microsoft, the U.S. Department of Justice begins its own antitrust investigation of Microsoft. In September, the European Community authorities begin an antitrust investigation of Microsoft's licensing practices.

In August 1994, Microsoft reaches a settlement with the U.S. Department of Justice regarding alleged monopolistic licensing practices. Microsoft agrees to change some of its practices in selling its operating systems to vendors in the United States and Europe. The Department of Justice begins the formal process of taking action against Microsoft.

In April, Gateway 2000 ships its 1 millionth PC since its founding in 1985.

The game Myst is released in June.

An article by Mike Feibus in *Microprocessor Report* calls the EPA's Energy Star initiative "a marketing gimmick with about as much meaning as a 'Lite' label on a package of bacon."

AT&T buys Go, which created software for mobile computers, and merges it into Eo.

At the 45th Annual Primetime Emmy Awards, the Academy of Television Arts and Sciences awards the Video Toaster's designers and NewTek's president an Emmy for developments in television engineering.

America Online releases America Online software for Windows.

In November, Benny S. Lee, of Everex Systems, Inc., is sentenced to one year in prison for manufacturing and selling counterfeit MS-DOS software. This is the first time a prison sentence is handed down for software counterfeiting in the United States.

1994

In January, Microsoft offers Netscape Communications US$1 million to license its browser code. James Clark declines the offer.

Seagate introduces a disk drive with a transfer rate of more than 100 megabytes per second.

Novell buys WordPerfect Corporation for US$850 million.

Commodore International and Commodore Electronics (two of the many international components of Commodore Business Machines) file for voluntary liquidation.

The National Science Foundation announces its intention to cease subsidies for the Internet backbone by May 1995, thus initiating a wave of privatization of this by-then-common good.

In June, Intel acknowledges the discovery, made a month earlier by Dr. Thomas R. Nicely of Lynchburg College, that the Pentium processor sometimes produces flawed floating-point results, yielding only 4 to 8 decimals of precision; Intel later confirms that about 2 million Pentium chips have been shipped with this defective unit, leading to suspension of all bugged PCs; the cost of destroying some 5 million flawed Pentium chips is estimated at US$475 million.

The first MacWorld Expo is held in San Francisco.

1995

The DVD (digital versatile disk), capable of storing eight times the capacity of the most powerful CD, is introduced.

MP3, Real Audio, and MPEG enable distribution of digital music and video.

Microsoft unveils Microsoft Bob, a "superapplication" with a "social interface" for Windows consumer users. Six months after its release, 30,000 units of Microsoft Bob have been sold.

An industry group (including such "heavyweights" as Compaq Computer, Digital Equipment, IBM, Intel, Microsoft, NEC, and Northern Telecom) forms the USB Implementers Forum, to develop a universal serial bus for personal computers.

In April, Netscape Communications releases the Netscape Navigator 1.1 Web browser.

The first macro virus program for Windows appears, called Concept.

In July, Microsoft stock hits US$100 per share.

On August 24, Microsoft releases Windows 95, Microsoft Office 95, and its Plus pack (which includes the Internet Explorer 1.0 Web browser), with a product launch in a circus tent on Microsoft's campus in Redmond, at a cost of US$200 million for the publicity campaign, including US$12 million for the rights to the Rolling Stones song "Start Me Up." On the first day of sales, some 300,000 copies are sold; by day 4 the number has reached 1 million copies.

IBM, Microsoft, Symantec, and others license Java from Sun Microsystems; Java allows various computing systems to use the same software.

The DVD Consortium is formed by Matsushita, Toshiba, Hitachi, JVC, Pioneer, Kodak, Mitsubishi, Philips, Thompson Multimedia, and Sony.

Estimated software industry losses to piracy in the United States for the year: US$2.9 billion; estimated worldwide software industry losses to piracy for the year: US$13.1 billion; rates of piracy for the year: Vietnam 99%, El Salvador 97%, China 96%, eastern Europe 83%, United States 26%.

1996

Sponsored by Microsoft and Compaq, a Chinese situation comedy called *My Computer Family* airs. Among other things, the show introduces the use of Microsoft products and the notion of the importance of intellectual property rights.

In May, the first JavaOne developers' conference is held, a gathering of over 6,000 people.

In December, a New York jury awards US$5.3 million to a secretary who claims that a Digital Equipment computer keyboard injured her wrists, thus launching a spin-off "industry" of ergonomics.

A computational record is broken on December 17: at the Sandia National Laboratory in Albuquerque, New Mexico, an Intel supercomputer performs 1 trillion floating-point operations per second.

1997

Wireless application protocol (WAP) is developed.

In June, Steve Jobs sells 1.5 million shares of Apple Computer stock, shares that he received in December as part of Apple Computer's purchase of his NeXT Software; the value of Apple Computer's stock drops to an 11-year low, leading to the resignation of Chairman and CEO Gil Amelios (with a severance package of some US$7.5 million).

The DVD Forum approves the DVD-RAM standard.

Sun Microsystems and Microsoft get into legal battles over the shipping of Microsoft's Internet Explorer 4.0 with a nonstandard implementation of the Java programming language; a month later, Microsoft releases an updated Microsoft Internet Explorer 4.01. By December, the market share of Web browser software is Netscape Navigator 54.6% and Microsoft Internet Explorer 29.5%; by the following August, the market is rearranged: Microsoft Internet Explorer at 75% of market share and Netscape Navigator at 23%.

Bell Laboratories in New Jersey announces that it has developed a 60-nanometer MOS transistor that is five times faster and one quarter the size of the current transistor and uses 60 to 160 times less power.

IBM's Austin Research Lab runs the world's first 1-GHz microprocessor.

1998

iMac, the newest, most powerful, and most stylish member of Apple products, appears on the market. By 2002, 6 million iMac machines have been sold.

In September, Microsoft becomes the world's most valuable company, at US$261.1 billion, by surpassing GE (both were valued at over US$300 billion in July, but Microsoft survived a stock market plunge better).

The *U.S. Department of Justice v. Microsoft* antitrust case begins, launching eight months of testimony alone.

America Online completes its acquisition of Netscape Communications.

December estimates show that the number of PCs in use worldwide is 364.4 million; 129 million PCs are in use in the United States alone. Also, some 45% of U.S. households own a personal computer.

1999

Microsoft introduces the IntelliMouse Explorer mouse, operating via an optical sensor rather than a rolling ball.

eMachines releases the eMachines eOne personal computer.

Apple's iBook comes on the market.

On November 5, Judge Thomas Jackson issues his findings of fact, ruling that Microsoft has monopoly power over personal computer operating systems and uses the power to harm American consumers; six months later, the judge issues his conclusions of law, affirming government charges that Microsoft used illegal practices to maintain its monopoly position, later ordering the breakup on Microsoft into two companies (one producing operating systems, the other producing application programs). The antitrust case is negotiated in a settlement in November 2001.

2000

In January, the U.S. Postal Service issues a 33-cent postage stamp depicting personal computers, part of its series of memories of the 1980s.

Larry Ellison unveils the New Internet Computer (NIC), developed by the New Internet Computer Company, at a price of US$199.

By April, IBM has shipped the 10 millionth ThinkPad portable computer.

On May 3, the computer virus Love Letter infects as many as 55 million personal computers around the world in about six hours, costing an estimated US$8.7 billion of downtime.

On September 14, Microsoft starts shipping the Windows Millennium Edition (Me) operating system.

The Federal Trade Commission closes its antitrust investigation of Intel, which started in September 1997, concluding that no action is required at this time.

The Y2K crisis is averted.

2001

Motorola is the first to introduce a complete portfolio of General Packet Radio Service (GPRS) wireless telephones that offer consumers always-on access to the Internet.

During the year, 124 to 134 million personal computers are sold worldwide.

2002

By May, about 1 billion PCs have been shipped worldwide.

Hewlett-Packard and Compaq Computer merge.

By June, the number of public, easily accessible sites on the World Wide Web has grown to approximately 3,080,000, or 1.4 billion Web pages. It is estimated that the static HTML text on the Web is equivalent to about 1.5 million books.

A federal judge orders Microsoft to include Sun Microsystems' Java in Windows.

2003

The number of secure Internet servers grows to 217,255; 210,134 of them are in high-income countries.

American citizens grow to accept e-government initiatives: 77% of American Internet users seek information on Web sites of local, state, and federal government, compared with 56% in 2002 and 47% in 2000.

Tim Berners-Lee is knighted in recognition of his creation of the World Wide Web.

2004

By September, of the 801.4 million on-line Internet users, the share of native speakers of English has shrunk to 35.2%.

"Year of the blog": blogging expands dramatically. By November, 27% of the 120 million adult Internet users in the United States read blogs, up from 17% only nine months earlier.

By year's end, 55% of all U.S. at-home Internet users and over 35% of users in the United Kingdom use broadband connections, as do over 150 million people worldwide.

2005

By January, the number of Internet hosts worldwide is estimated at 317,646,084, having grown by almost 50% since the previous year.

Short Message Service (SMS) hits cell phone users, particularly the Y generation (ages 18–27), 63% of whom use SMS on their cell phones. Only 31% of generation X (ages 28–39), 18% of baby boomers (ages 40–49), 13% of people ages 5–59, and 7% of people over age 60 use SMS.

Bill Gates, Microsoft's cofounder and chairman and the world's wealthiest man, is knighted.

By March, only 13.9% of the world's total populations are Internet users: 67.4% of the total population in North America, 48% in Australia and Oceania, 35.5% in Europe, 10.3% in Latin America and the Caribbean, 8.4% in Asia, 7.5% in the Middle East, and 1.5% in Africa.

In March, the Microsoft Windows family accounts for 90.3% of all operating systems in use, with Windows XP alone accounting for a 63.1% share.

By the end of March, there are 2,294,136,335 registered IP addresses worldwide, 57% in United States alone.

Technical Glossary

For clarification of other Internet terms, see any one of the various Internet glossaries listed on http://www.isoc.org/internet/links/glossaries.shtml.

ASCII American Standard Code for Information Interchange; basic form of text (also referred to as "plain text" or "vanilla text"), which allows for easy exchange across platforms. Therefore, all e-mail messages are transmitted over the Internet in ASCII form.

bandwidth Measure of the capacity of the network to transmit data within a fixed time unit; for example, for digital systems it quantifies the number of bytes per second. It thus appraises the ability of the network to operate multiple major tasks: to serve multiple users, to transfer great amounts of data, and to execute these tasks simultaneously.

blog Shorthand for Web log, a publicly accessible journal as logged by an individual or a group. Blogs on a particular topic are kept in sequential accounts.

bus Channel over which information flows between two or more devices, within or between digital components; technically, a bus has only two devices or it is considered by some a port. A bus normally has access points, or places into which a device can tap to become part of the bus, and devices on the bus can send to and receive information from other devices.

CTR Cathode ray tube. Used in display monitors of television sets and in computer screens to project a picture. A rapidly moving electron beam reacts with the phosphor dots inside the tube.

e-mail Electronic mail; mail exchanges transferred digitally between computers.

GB/s Gigabytes per second. A measure of capacity of data transfer per unit of time for digital systems.

HTML HyperText Markup Language. The computer language used to compose documents on the World Wide Web. Through a variety of tags and attributes (such as <HTML> <HEAD>, which is used to start each document or page), HTML organizes a Web page and refers the user to other links.

HTTP HyperText Transfer Protocol. The protocol used on the World Wide Web to define how messages are formatted and transmitted and what Web browsers do in response to these commands. For example, HTTP is the command format that directs the computer to display a Web page in reaction to a **URL** entry.

Internet host Independent Internet node with an Internet Protocol (IP) address. Hosts are labeled by a 32-byte numerical sequence (sectioned into four groups divided by periods); an example is 01.23.456.789. Each host also has a **URL**.

LAN Local-area network, set up within the parameters of an organization and among its members.

MIDI Musical Instrument Digital Interface. Industry standard electronic interface that links electronic music synthesizers. The MIDI information tells a synthesizer when to start and stop playing a specific note, what sound the note should have, how loud it should be, and other information.

MS-DOS Microsoft Disk Operating System. Originally developed by Microsoft for IBM, this operating system served all IBM-compatible PCs. Because of its inability to serve multiple users or support multitasking, MS-DOS was eventually replaced by the Microsoft Windows platform.

SMS Short Message Service. Similar to paging; allows sending short text messages between cellular phones, fax machines, and IP addresses. Text messages are limited to less than 160 alphanumeric characters and do not allow graphics.

URL Uniform—or Universal—Resource Locator. Internet address used in Hypertext—the familiar http://www addresses.

Worm Short program that searches a network for idle processors. Initially designed to provide more efficient use of computers and for testing, the worm had the unintended effect of invading networked computers, creating a security threat.

WWW World Wide Web. Hypertext platforms that link the public files of computers that have set up home pages.

General Abbreviations

BAN	Basel action network
ICANN	Internet Corporation for Assigned Names and Numbers
IP	Intellectual property
GATT	General Agreement on Tariffs and Trade
GDP	Gross domestic product
GNP	Gross national product
ICT	Information and communications technology
IGO	International government organization
INGO	International nongovernment organization
ITU	International Telecommunication Union
MDG	Millennium Development Goals
NICs	Newly industrialized countries
OECD	Organisation for Economic Co-operation and Development
R&D	Research and development
TAI	Technology Achievement Index
TRIPS	Trade-related aspects of intellectual property agreement
UNDP	United Nations Development Programme
UNESCO	United Nations Education, Science and Culture Organization
WIPO	World Intellectual Property Organization
WTO	World Trade Organization

Bibliography

Ackerman, Gwen. 2001. "Israel's Internet Don Quixote." *Jerusalem Post* (Digital Israel Section), June 5, 2001 (14 Sivan 5761). http://www.jpost. com/Editions/2001/06/03/Digital/Digital.27401.html, accessed April 14, 2002.

Alkalimat, Abdul. 2004. *The African American Experience in Cyberspace: A Resource Guide to the Best Web Sits on Black Culture and History.* London: Pluto Press.

Annan, Kofi. (2003). "Welcome Message to the World Summit on Information Society." Geneva. Available at http://www.dailysummit.net/ english/archives/2003/12/09/kofi-annan-speaks.asp.

Appadurai, Arjun. 1996. *Modernity at Large: Cultural Dimensions of Globalization.* Minneapolis: University of Minnesota Press.

Attewell, Paul. 2001. "The First and Second Digital Divides." *Sociology of Education* 74: 252–259.

Becker, Gary. 1964. *Human Capital.* New York: Columbia University Press.

Berners-Lee, Tim (with Mark Fischetti). 1999. *Weaving the Web: The Original Design and Ultimate Destiny of the World Wide Web by Its Inventor.* San Francisco: Harper.

"Beyond the Digital Divide." 2004 (March 13). *Economist Technology Quarterly,* p. 8.

Birdsell, David, Douglas Muzio, David Krane, and Amy Cottreau. 1998. "Web Users Are Looking More Like America." *The Public Perspective* 9(3): 33. www.roper-center.uconn.edu/pubpr/pp93.htm

Bush, Vannevar. 1945 (July). "As We May Think." *Atlantic Monthly.*

BusinessWeek. 2000 (May 8). "How to Bridge America's Digital Divide" (editorial).

Cammaerts, Bart, Leo Van Audenhove, Gert Nulens, and Caroline Pauwels (eds.). 2004. *Beyond the Digital Divide: Reducing Exclusion, Fostering Inclusion.* Brussels: Brussels University Press.

Castells, Manuel. (1996). *Volume 1: The Rise of the Network Society.* Oxford and Malden, MA: Blackwell.

Castells, Manuel. (1997). *Volume 2: The Power of Identity.* Oxford and Malden, MA: Blackwell.

Castells, Manuel. (1998). *Volume 3: End of Millenium*. Oxford and Malden, MA: Blackwell.

Compaine, Benjamin M. (ed.). 2001. *The Digital Divide: Facing a Crisis or Creating a Myth?* Cambridge, MA: MIT Press.

Crystal, David. 1997. *English as a Global Language*. New York: Cambridge University Press.

De Haan, Jos. 2003. "IT and Social Inequality in the Netherlands." *IT and Society* 1(4): 27–45.

DiMaggio, Paul, Eszter Hargittai, W. Russell Neuman, and John P. Robinson. 2001. "Social Implications of the Internet." *Annual Review of Sociology* 27: 307–336.

Drori, Gili S., and Yong Suk Jang. 2003. "The Global Digital Divide: A Sociological Assessment of Trends and Causes." *Social Science Computer Review* 21(2): 144–161.

Drori, Gili S., John W. Meyer, Francisco O. Ramirez, and Even Schofer. 2003. *Science in the Modern World Polity: Institutionalization and Globalization*. Stanford, CA: Stanford University Press.

Durham, Mercedes. 2003. "Language Choice on a Swiss Mailing List." *Journal of Computer-Mediated Communication* 9(1).

Fong, E., Barry Wellman, R. Wilkes, and M. Kew. 2001. *The Double Digital Divide*. Ottawa: Office of Learning Technologies, Human Resources Development Canada.

Foucault, Michel. 1980. *Power/Knowledge*. New York: Pantheon Press.

Foucault, Michel. 1991. "Governmentality." In Graham Burchell, Colin Gordon, and Peter Miller (eds.), *The Foucault Effect: Studies in Governmentality*, 87–104. Chicago: University of Chicago Press.

Giddens, Anthony. 1990. *The Consequences of Modernity*. Cambridge, UK: Polity.

Grusky, David B. 1994. *Social Stratification: Class, Race, and Gender in Sociological Perspective*. Boulder, CO: Westview Press.

Hammond, Allen L. 2001. "Digitally Empowered Development, *Foreign Affairs* 80(2). Available at www.foreignaffairs.org/2001/2.

Hardy, Jackie. 1999. "Computer-Aided Design." In Neil Astley (ed.), *New Blood*, p. 199. Newcastle upon Tyne, UK: Bloodaxe Books.

Harvey, David. 1989. *The Condition of Postmodernity*. Oxford: Blackwell.

International Telecommunication Union. 2001 (January/February/March). *Numbering Cyberspace: Recent Trends in the Internet World*. ITU Telecommunication Indicators Update. http://www.itu.int/ITU-D/ict/statistics, accessed October 31, 2002.

International Telecommunication Union. 2003. *World Telecommunication Development Report: Summary*. Geneva: ITU World Summit on the Information Society.

Internet Society. 1997 (June). "Web Languages Hit Parade." www.isoc.org:8080/palmares.en.html, accessed January 23, 2004.

James, Jeffrey. 2003. *Bridging the Global Digital Divide*. Cheltenham, UK: Edward Elgar.

Jorgenson, Dale. 2003 (October 25). "Information Technology and the G7 Economies," *Economist*, p. 70.

Kagami, Mitsuhiro, Masatsugu Tsuji, and Emanuele Giovannetti (eds.). 2004. *Information Technology Policy and the Digital Divide: Lessons for Developing Countries*. Oxford: Marston.

Kearney, A. T. 2003 (January/February). "Measuring Globalization: Who's Up, Who's Down?" *Foreign Policy*, 60–72.

Keniston, Kenneth. 2004. "Introduction: The Four Digital Divides." In Kenneth Keniston and Deepak Kumar (eds.), *IT Experience in India: Bridging the Digital Divide*, 11–36. New Delhi: Sage.

Kenney, Martin. 2003. "The Growth and Development of the Internet in the United States." In Bruce Kogut (ed.), *The Global Internet Economy*, 69–108. Cambridge, MA: MIT Press

Khasiani, Shanyisa Anota. 1999. "Enhancing Women's Participation in Governance: The Case of Kakamega and Makueni Districts, Kenya." In Eva-Maria Rathgeber and Edith Ofwona Adera (eds.), *Gender and the Information Revolution in Africa*. http://www.idrc/ca/books/focus/903/11-chp08.html, accessed December 28, 2004.

Kogut, Bruce (ed.). 2003. *Global Internet Economy*. Cambridge, MA: MIT Press.

Koutsogiannis, Dimitris, and Bessie Mitsikopoulou. 2003. "Greeklish and Greekness: Trends and Discourses of 'Glocalness.'" *Journal of Computer-Mediated Communication* 9(1). Available at http://www.ascusc.org/jcmc/vol9/issue1/kouts_mits.html.

Kozma, Robert, Ray McGhree, Edys Quellmalz, and Dan Zalels. 2004. "Closing the Digital Divide: Evaluation of the World Links Program." *International Journal of Educational Development* 24(4): 361–381.

Kumar, Harsh. 2004. "Science, Technology, and the Politics of Computers in Indian Languages." In Kenneth Keniston and Deepak Kumar (eds.), *IT Experience in India: Bridging the Digital Divide*, 11–36. New Delhi: Sage.

Kummer, Katharine. 1995. *International Management of Hazardous Wastes: The Basel Convention and Related Legal Rules.* Oxford: Clarendon Press.

Lee, Sherry. 2002 (May 12). "Ghosts in the Machines." *South China Morning Post Magazine.* Available at http://www.ban.org/Library/ghosts_in.html, accessed October 31, 2002.

Lenhart, Amanda, and John B. Horrigan. 2003. "Re-Visualizing the Digital Divide as a Digital Spectrum." *IT and Society* 1(5): 23–39.

Lenhart, Amanda, John Horrigan, Lee Rainie, Katherine Allen, Angie Boyce, Mary Madden, and Erin O'Grach. 2003. *The Ever-Shifting Internet Population: A New Look at Internet Access and the Digital Divide.* Washington, DC: Pew Internet and American Life Project.

Losh, Susan Carol. 2003a. "Gender and Educational Digital Chasms in Computer and Internet Access and Use over Time: 1983–2000." *IT and Society* 1(4): 73–86.

Losh, Susan Carol. 2003b. "Gender and Educational Digital Gaps." *IT and Society* 1(5): 56–71.

Main, Linda. 2001. "The Global Information Infrastructure: Empowerment or Imperialism?" *Third World Development* 22(1): 83–97.

Mato, Daniel. 2000. "Transnational Networking and the Social Production of Representations of Identities by Indigenous Peoples' Organizations in Latin America." *International Sociology* 15(2): 343–360.

Miller, Marian A. L. 1995. *The Third World in Global Environmental Politics.* Boulder, CO: Lynne Reinner.

Mitter, Swasti, and Sheila Rowbotham (eds.). 1995. *Women Encounter Technology: Changing Patterns of Employment in the Third World.* London: Routledge.

Mossberger, Karen, Caroline J. Tolbert, and Mary Stansbury. 2003. *Virtual Inequality: Beyond the Digital Divide.* Washington, DC: Georgetown University Press.

Mueller, M. L. 2001. "Universal Service Policies and Wealth Redistribution." In Benjamin M. Compaine (ed.), *The Digital Divide: Facing a Crisis or Creating a Myth?* 179–187. Cambridge, MA: MIT Press.

Myers, J. 1998. "Human Rights and Development: Using Advance Technology to Promote Human Rights in Sub-Saharan Africa." *Case Western Reserve Journal of International Law* 30(2/3): 343–371.

Namibia Ministry of Education, Culture and Sport. 2002. "Education for All Plan of Action." Windhoek, Namibia.

National Public Radio. 1999 (November 30). *Talk of the Nation.*

National Research Council. 1999. *Being Fluent with Information Technology.* Washington, DC: National Academy Press.

National Telecommunications and Information Administration. 1995. "Falling through the Net: A Survey of the 'Have-Nots' in Rural and Urban America." Washington, DC: U.S. Department of Commerce, NTIA. Available at www.ntia.doc.gov/ntiahome/digitaldivide.

National Telecommunications and Information Administration. 1998. "Falling through the Net: New Data on the Digital Divide." Washington, DC: U.S. Department of Commerce, NTIA. Available at www.ntia. doc.gov/ntiahome/digitaldivide.

National Telecommunications and Information Administration. 1999. "Falling through the Net: Defining the Digital Divide." Washington, DC: NTIA. Available at www.ntia.doc.gov/ntiahome/digitaldivide.

National Telecommunications and Information Administration. 2000. "Falling through the Net: Towards Digital Inclusion." Washington, DC: U.S. Department of Commerce, NTIA. Available at www.ntia.doc.gov/ ntiahome/digitaldivide.

Noble, David F. 1993. *Progress without People: In Defense of Luddism.* Chicago: Kerr.

Noble, David F. 2002. *Digital Diploma Mills: The Automation of Higher Education.* New York: Monthly Review Press.

Norr, Henry. 2001 (May 27). "Drowning in e-Waste: Safe Disposal of Mountains of Old PCs, Monitors Is a Snowballing Problem We've Only Begun to Face." *San Francisco Chronicle.* http://www.sfgate.com/cgi-bin/ article.cgi?file= percent2Fchronicle percent2Farchive percent2F2001 percent2F05 percent2F27 percent2FBU119228 percent2EDTL

Norris, Pipa, W. Lance Bennett, and Robert M. Entman. 2001. *Digital Divide: Civic Engagement, Information Poverty, and the Internet Worldwide.* Cambridge, UK: Cambridge University Press.

Nulens, Gret, Nancy Hafkin, Leo Van Audenhove, and Bart Cammaerts (eds.). 2001. *The Digital Divide in Developing Countries: An Information Society in Africa.* Brussels: Brussels University Press.

Nunberg, Geoffrey. 2000 (March 27). "Will the Internet Always Speak English?" *American Prospect* 11(10). Available at www.prospect.org.

Opoku-Mensah, Aida. 2004. "Twin Peaks: WSIS from Geneva to Tunis." *Gazette: The International Journal for Communication Studies* 66(3–4): 256.

Organisation for Economic Co-operation and Development. 2000. *Information Technology Outlook.* Paris: OECD.

Organisation for Economic Co-operation and Development. 2001. "ICT Investment and Economic Growth in the 1990s: Is the US a Unique Case? A Comparative Study of 9 OECD Countries." Working paper 2001/7. Paris: OECD Directorate for Science, Technology and Industry. Available at http://www.olis.oecd.org/olis/2001doc.nsf/LinkTo/DSTI-DOC(2001)7, accessed February 3, 2004.

Phillipson, Robert. 1992. *Linguistic Imperialism.* Oxford: Oxford University Press.

Phillipson, Robert. 2003. *English-Only Europe? Challenging Language Policy.* London: Routledge.

Price, Monroe E. 2002. *Media and Sovereignty: The Global Information Revolution and Its Challenges to State Power,* Cambridge, MA: MIT Press.

Qureshi, Sajda. 1998. "Fostering Civil Associations in Africa through GOVERNET: An Administrative Reform Network." *Journal of Information Technology for Development* 8: 121–136.

Raja, M. (2004, April 6). "E-Wasting Away in India." *Asia Times Online.* http://www.atimes.com/atimes/South_Asia/FD06Df02.html, accessed April 24, 2004.

Ritzer, George. 2004. *The Globalization of Nothing.* Thousand Oaks, CA: Pine Forge.

Robertson, Roland. 1992. *Globalization: Social Theory and Global Culture.* London: Sage.

Robertson, Roland. 1994. "Globalization and Glocalization." *Journal of International Communications* 1(1): 33–52.

Sachs, Jeffrey, 2000 (June 24). "A New Map of the World." *Economist.*

Sako, Marie. "Between Bit Valley and Silicon Valley: Hybrid Forms of Business Governance in the Japanese Internet Economy." In Bruce Kogut (ed.), *The Global Internet Economy.* Cambridge, MA: MIT Press.

Sale, Kirkpatrick. 1995 (June). Interview. *Wired* 3(6).

Sassen, Saskia. 1996. "The Spatial Organization of Information Industries: Implications for the Role of the State." In James H. Mittleman (ed.), *Globalization: Critical Reflections,* 33–52. Boulder, CO: Lynne Rienner.

Schultz, Theodore W. 1961. "Investment in Human Capital." *American Economic Review* 51(10): 1–16.

Selwyn, Neil. 2002. "E-Stablishing an Inclusive Society? Technology, Social Exclusion and UK Government Policy-Making." *Journal of Social Policy* 31: 1–20.

Thurow, Lester. 1996. *The Future of Capitalism: How Today's Economic Forces Shape Tomorrow's World.* New York: Morrow.

Tilly, Charles. 1999. *Durable Inequalities.* Berkeley, CA: University of California Press.

UNESCO. 1999. "Declaration on Science and the Use of Scientific Knowledge," Section 33. World Conference on Science for the 21st Century, Budapest. Available at www.unesco.org/science/wcs/eng/declaration_e.htm.

United Nations (2000). "Millennium Development Goals." New York: United Nations. Available at www.un.org/milleniumgoals/.

United Nations Development Programme. 2001. *Human Development Report 2001: Making New Technologies Work for Human Development.* New York: UNDP.

United Nations Development Programme. 2002. *Human Development Report 2001: Deepening Democracy in a Fragmented World.* New York: UNDP.

United Nations Development Programme. 2004. *Human Development Report 2004: Cultural Liberty in Today's Diverse World.* New York: UNDP.

Van Dijk, Jan. 1999. *The Network Society.* London: Sage.

Waters, Malcolm. 1995. *Globalization.* London: Routledge.

Wilkes, M. V. 1985. *Memoirs of a Computer Pioneer.* Cambridge, MA: MIT Press.

Wilkinson, Kenton T. 2004. "Language Differences and Communications Policy in the Information Age." *Information Society* 20: 220.

World Bank. 2000. *World Development Indicators.* CD-ROM and http://www.worldbank.org/data/wdi/index.htm.

World Bank. 2004. *2004 Development Indicators.* Washington DC: World Bank.

Index